CREATED FOR MORE

30 Days to Seeing Your World in a New Way

Jonathan Malm

D1167268

MOODY PUBLISHERS
CHICAGO

All Scripture quotations, unless otherwise indicated, are taken from the Holy Bible, New Living Translation, copyright © 1996, 2004. Used by permission of Tyndale House Publishers, Inc., Wheaton, Illinois 60189, U.S.A. All rights reserved. All italics shown in Scripture quotations have been placed there by the author.

All Scripture quotations marked MSG are taken from The Message, copyright © by Eugene H. Peterson 1993, 1994, 1995. Used by permission of NavPress Publishing Group.

All Scripture quotations marked NASB are taken from the New American Standard Bible®, Copyright © 1960, 1962, 1963, 1968, 1971, 1972, 1973, 1975, 1977, 1995 by The Lockman Foundation. Used by permission. (www.Lockman.org)

All Scripture quotations marked ESV are taken from The Holy Bible, English Standard Version. Copyright © 2000, 2001 by Crossway Bibles, a division of Good News Publishers. Used by permission. All rights reserved.

All Scripture quotations marked KJV are taken from the King James Version.

All Scripture quotations marked NET are taken from the New English Translation Bible. Copyright © 2005 by Biblical Studies Press, LLC.

All Scripture quotations marked CEB are taken from the Common English Bible. Copyright © 2010 by Christian Resources Development Corporation.

All Scripture quotations marked ASV are taken from the American Standard Version. Copyright © 1901, 1929 by Gospel Light Publishing Company.

All Scripture quotations marked NLV are taken from the New Life Version. Copyright © 1986 by Christian Literature International.

Edited by Jesse Lipes
Interior design: Design Corps
Cover design: Simplicated Studio
Cover image: Rhythms photo: Mophoto / Photographer Dillon Klassen
          Musical score: iStock photo #2783624
          Brushing on paper: iStock photo #10795516

Library of Congress Cataloging-in-Publication Data
Malm, Jonathan.
  Created for more : 30 days to seeing your world in a new way / by Jonathan Malm.
    pages cm
  ISBN 978-0-8024-1219-5
  1. Christian life--Meditations. 2. Spiritual exercises. 3. Christian philosophy--Meditations.
  I. Title.
  BV4832.3.M33 2014
  242'.2--dc23

                    2014011184

We hope you enjoy this book from Moody Publishers. Our goal is to provide high-quality, thought-provoking books and products that connect truth to your real needs and challenges. For more information on other books and products written and produced from a biblical perspective, go to **www.moodypublishers.com** or write to:

Moody Publishers
820 N. LaSalle Boulevard
Chicago, IL 60610

1 3 5 7 9 10 8 6 4 2

Printed in the United States of America

PRAISE FOR

Created for More

JONATHAN HAS PUT TOGETHER a great devotional for anyone who wants to see their world in a unique way. Whether you're creative or even part creative, this book will help you grow in both your craft and your walk with God—in only 30 days!

Mark Batterson, *New York Times* bestselling author of *The Circle Maker* and lead pastor of National Community Church in Washington, DC

JONATHAN MALM IS ONE of the most creative, faith-filled people I know. You'll find no better guide to help you discover your great gift to the world.

Ben Arment, author of *Dream Year*

I'M OF THE OPINION that better humans make better art. I'm also of the opinion that after 30 days with Jonathan's thoughts you'll be better at both. A simple, yet provocative journey through Scripture and the creative mind, this devotional is one worth reading.

Blaine Hogan, creative director at Willow Creek Community Church

CREATED FOR MORE WAS CREATED with you in mind! This devotional is Jonathan Malm's heartbeat. His passion to help awaken the spiritual act of creativity within each of us is evidenced throughout these pages. This will be a valuable resource not only for you but also for the teams of creatives you lead.

Jenni Catron, church leader and author of *CLOUT: Discover and Unleash Your God-Given Influence*

Dedication

"Surround yourself with the dreamers and the doers, the believers and thinkers, but most of all, surround yourself with those who see the greatness within you, even when you don't see it yourself." —EDMUND LEE

This book is dedicated to the dreamers and the doers, the believers and thinkers, but most of all, to those who see greatness in us, even when we don't see it ourselves.

CONTENTS

INTRODUCTION   9

DAY	BE...	PAGE	DAY	BE...	PAGE
1	Be Humble	13	16	Be Content	62
2	Be Limited	17	17	Be Great	66
3	Be a Dancer	21	18	Be Perceptive	70
4	Be Intentional	24	19	Be Parallel	74
5	Be Curious	28	20	Be Incomparable	78
6	Be Tenacious	31	21	Be Different	81
7	Be Redemptive	34	22	Be Associated	84
8	Be Invested	37	23	Be Determined	88
9	Be Resisted	40	24	Be Long-suffering	91
10	Be Liberal	43	25	Be Secure	95
11	Be Brave	46	26	Be Defeated	98
12	Be Dual	49	27	Be Generous	101
13	Be Prepared	53	28	Be Dedicated	104
14	Be Fresh	56	29	Be Bold	107
15	Be Relaxed	59	30	Be Light	110

APPENDIXES	A	50 What Ifs	113
	B	Tracking Your Progress	117

NOTES   119

ACKNOWLEDGMENTS   121

INTRODUCTION

HERE'S MY CONFESSION. I'VE halfway read dozens of devotional books. When I start to read a new devotional, I have the best of intentions. I truly want to follow through and finish it. Somewhere in the process my interest level drops and the book finds its way to the devotional graveyard on my bookshelf.

It's hard for me to stick with a devotional. My brain is prone to wander and imagine. I need variety. I need mystery. I need something that will hold my short attention span. Do you relate?

I wrote this to help us get out of our communal rut. You might feel stuck in your job, in your relationships, or in your thought processes. This devotional is meant to help you see both your work and your world differently. It's meant to help you read the Bible differently.

The Bible is an incredibly creative book. It's filled with stories and inspiration that speak to your daily life. To the things you make. Whether you're a graphic designer, a carpenter, a painter, a singer, a dancer, a marketing executive, a barista, a photographer . . . if you are involved in making something, creative thinking will help you do it better. The Bible is absolutely filled with creative thoughts.

The goal for these next thirty days will be to help you on the journey out of your rut and toward doing better work.

It explores the conjunction of the Bible, your spiritual walk, and your creative potential.

The act of creativity reflects our creative God. Everything we see was designed by our Creator. He saw that what He made was good. And when we make things, we share in that goodness. He's given us the opportunity to work with our hands and see the fruit of our labor. What an amazing opportunity.

The act of producing things is a very spiritual thing. Too often we make it about ourselves. We focus on our emotions, our talents, or our personality. We make it completely about ourselves when it's really a chance to commune with and experience the very nature of God. He has given us the chance and the drive to be part of something bigger than ourselves.

I need something different. I need a devotional that speaks to my artistic side as well as my spiritual side.

That's why I wrote *Created for More*—to help awaken the spiritual act of creativity within myself and within you, to honor and develop the hunger inside you to make something good. I want to help you see the world differently and approach your problems in fresh, new ways by suggesting practical steps that will make the work of your hands more productive and effective. You don't have to feel stuck in a rut. There's a creative way to get out. Let's explore it together.

As we explore this new way of thinking, I encourage you to set a schedule for reading and completing the challenges in this book. This can be a one-month, a six-week, or a one-year journey. Choose a reading schedule that suits your schedule—one every day, one every weekday, or one every week. Use this as a chance to commune with God and the unique nature He's placed inside you. Do the challenges and pray the included prayers. Don't worry: it will only take a few minutes each day.

I encourage you to keep track of your journey. Blog the results of your challenges. Tweet your own thoughts or the thought of the day. Then follow how others are engaging with *Created for More*.

You can follow and use the hashtag #createdformore on Twitter and Instagram. Then post and read from others on createdformore.me.

My prayer is that you'll develop both as a follower of Christ and as someone who creates things through this journey of devotion and creation.

BE HUMBLE

*The best work comes when
we don't take ourselves
too seriously.*

Spiritual Development

**Now, O people, the LORD has told you what is good,
and this is what he requires of you: to do what is
right, to love mercy, and to walk humbly with your
God.**

MICAH 6:8

WHAT DOES GOD REQUIRE of us? Only three things. Do right.
Love mercy. Walk humbly with our God.

There's a lot packed in those three statements. Let's focus on that third one: walking humbly. Humility.

Many of us see humility as a masochistic act. If we beat
ourselves down enough and think lowly enough of ourselves,
we achieve humility. So we walk around with frail self-esteem

and a fear of putting ourselves out there. We don't want to seem proud, after all.

Artists—especially in the church—are geniuses at this masochistic humility. I used to excel at this. When I'd hop off the stage after leading worship, I'd almost stiff arm any compliment heading my way. And when I wasn't repelling the compliments, one of the pastors on staff made it his business to keep me humble.

There are far too many downtrodden and frail artists in the church. That's not what humility is about.

I love how The Message paraphrases the last part of our verse: "And don't take yourself too seriously—take God seriously."

That's humility! Chill out and don't be self-absorbed. When we take God seriously it stops being about us and starts being about Him. It's no longer about our ego but about His glory.

But so often we take ourselves too seriously.

We've all seen the obvious example of this. I'm sure you've had a friend or two who are minefields. You have to tiptoe through your conversations for fear of upsetting the delicate balance of their psyche and setting them off. If you touch on the wrong topics or say the wrong things, they explode!

They're obviously taking themselves too seriously. That's not humility.

A less obvious example is the bashful artist. They're afraid to put themselves out there because they're afraid of what people will think. "What if they hate my work and reject me?"

They, too, are taking themselves too seriously.

When God calls us to do something, we have no business being bashful. Think of Jesus—the ultimate example of humility. He wasn't bashful about speaking to the thousands. He wasn't bashful about telling us to be holy like He is holy. He wasn't even afraid to demonstrate His humility with words. He was and is humble.

Humility is not thinking less of yourself. It's thinking of yourself less. It's having an accurate picture of yourself and realizing it ultimately doesn't matter. Only what glorifies God matters. Humility is taking God seriously without taking ourselves too seriously.

So it's time for a life checkup. How are you doing at walking humbly with your God? Are you taking yourself too seriously? Are you worried more about your ego than about doing what God's called you to do?

Prayer Starter

God, I choose to start taking You seriously. I'm tired of taking myself too seriously. Help me to walk humbly before You and to do what You've called me to do. Help me have an accurate picture of myself and realize it ultimately doesn't matter. You matter.

Change the Way You Think

Now to your work. Have you been confusing humility for self-deprecation? Perhaps the leaders in your life have even led you to believe that's what humility means.

Clear that false idea from your mind. It will only taint what God called you to do. If you're an artist, He called you to create. If you're a writer, He called you to write. If you're a speaker, He called you to speak. Do everything without holding back.

Our best work comes when we don't take ourselves too seriously. It allows us to take risks. To be brave. To try something new. We're willing to explore and to bring others into the exploration with us.

The world desperately needs people who know what it means to be humble. Stop taking yourself seriously and start taking God seriously.

Challenge

Whatever your unique outlet, create something intentionally horrible. And have fun doing it! Then share it with your friends and family. Let them enjoy the atrocity.

Don't take yourself seriously as you create. You might just find some beauty or a new technique you hadn't discovered previously.

BE LIMITED

> *Limitations force
> creative solutions.*

Spiritual Development

GOD said to Gideon, "You have too large an army with you. I can't turn Midian over to them like this—they'll take all the credit, saying, 'I did it all myself,' and forget about me. Make a public announcement: 'Anyone afraid, anyone who has any qualms at all, may leave Mount Gilead now and go home.'"

Twenty-two companies headed for home. Ten companies were left.

GOD said to Gideon: "There are still too many. Take them down to the stream and I'll make a final cut. When I say, 'This one goes with you,' he'll go. When I say, 'This one doesn't go,' he won't go." So Gideon took the troops down to the stream.

GOD said to Gideon: "Everyone who laps with his tongue, the way a dog laps, set on one side. And everyone who kneels to drink, drinking with his face to the water, set to the other side." Three hundred lapped with their tongues from their cupped hands. All the rest knelt to drink.

> GOD said to Gideon: "I'll use the three hundred
> men who lapped at the stream to save you and give
> Midian into your hands. All the rest may go home."
>
> JUDGES 7:2–7 (MSG)

GIDEON WAS CALLED TO fight a battle. Gideon and the Israelite army were grossly outnumbered: 32,000 Israelite troops to 135,000 Midianite troops. And if that wasn't enough, God shrank Gideon's army down to 300!

Imagine Gideon's terror. This battle was a matter of life and death. And God wanted to limit Gideon's army to only 300? But God had a plan—a creative plan.

Through a bit of crazy misdirection and some shock-and-awe antics, the Midian army defeated themselves! Hollywood script writers still struggle to invent clever plot lines like this! The Midianite army got confused, and they literally turned on each other. Then the battle was over.

300 men + God's creative plan = victory.

The coolest part about the creative plan was this: no Israelite casualties. If Gideon had stormed the enemy with his 32,000 troops, he would have lost many men. Even if he'd done it with 500,000 men, the losses would have been devastating. Our creative God—by limiting the army to 300—forced an outside-the-box idea. And God got the glory.

Many of us equate limitations with hindrances. When we don't have enough time, finances, or resources, we resort to complaining and wishing we had more. But God has given you everything you need to do His will. When we're willing to work within the limitations and we find success, He gets the glory—not us.

That's what life is all about—bringing glory to God. So why should we worry when there isn't enough money in the bank account? Why should we complain when we don't have all the resources we think we need?

Give the situation to God and let His creativity take over. Trust Him completely and let Him do something awe-inspiring in your life.

Prayer Starter

God, I choose to see limitations as an opportunity rather than a hindrance. Instead of complaining or wishing for more, I want to trust that You can do the miraculous and intervene. You can take my limitations and do something amazing with them. You are the author of all creativity and there is nothing beyond Your grasp. I trust in You.

Change the Way You Think

There's such beauty in this story for those of us who make things. It illustrates an amazing facet of creativity—limitations force creative solutions.

This would be a completely unremarkable story if Gideon had the resources he thought he needed. Anyone can win a battle with a well-staffed, well-funded army. Because when the going gets tough you simply throw more resources in the mix. No creativity needed.

The same is true for what you produce. If you had all the necessary resources at your fingertips, you wouldn't be forced to think creatively or outside the box. Consider an advertising executive with a multimillion dollar budget. Instead of relying on creativity for his ads, he hires ten celebrity spokesmen. These ads simply fade into the white noise of endorsements featuring celebrities. Instead, when you think of some of the most famous ad campaigns, they didn't rely on big budgets. They relied on creativity.

Limitations force creative solutions.

So instead of complaining about your lack of resources today, look at the opportunity for creativity. You might even avoid some proverbial casualties in the process.

Challenge

Choose one project you're working on. Then cut your resources for that project in half. Move your deadline closer. Cut the budget. Remove some technological resources. Create some limitations.

Now think creatively. Look for unique ways to accomplish the same goal. Decide what's really necessary for the project. You'll find many of the resources were unnecessary for accomplishing your goal.

BE A DANCER

> *A life of meaning is dynamic.*
> *It can't always be lived in*
> *neat, straight lines.*

Spiritual Development

The Holy Spirit kept them from preaching the Word of God in the countries of Asia. When they came to the city of Mysia, they tried to go on to the city of Bithynia but the Holy Spirit would not let them go. From Mysia they went down to the city of Troas. That night Paul had a dream. A man was standing in front of him crying out, "Come over to the country of Macedonia and help us!"

After he had seen this, we agreed that God told us to go to Macedonia to tell them the Good News.

ACTS 16:6–10 (NLV)

THE APOSTLE PAUL AND his entourage were on their missionary journey. They were trying to decide where to go next. The above passage makes it seem as if their progress was a lot like a pinball machine. They headed to one region, then hit a wall. So they bounced on to the next location. Another wall. They bounced on and on until Paul finally had a dream. That's when they finally realized where they needed to go.

Imagine how frustrating that would have been! They felt called by God to preach the gospel, but they kept meeting with resistance. That resistance was the Holy Spirit Himself. I know they got discouraged. They were people, just like you and me. They got discouraged, but they still obeyed.

When things like this happen to us, we can choose to see it in one of two ways. We can either see God playing games with us like we're in a pinball machine, or we can see God dancing with us.

I encourage you to see it like a dance.

Good dancing requires a leader and a follower. God is a great leader. How are we at following?

If the follower chooses to take control, the dance can easily fall apart. That's when people's toes get stepped on. That's when folks bump into each other. There must be a leader and a follower. And God will not follow.

But when the follower chooses to trust the leader, the dance becomes beautiful. It becomes exciting and unpredictable. There's harmony and beauty.

So as you follow God, I encourage you to dance. Don't get discouraged when God takes you in a new direction. He knows the music and He knows where we need to be. Follow Him and He'll take you there. It will be beautiful.

The world is a dance floor. God wants to dance with you. Will you let Him take the lead?

Prayer Starter

God, I choose to trust You in this dance. I choose to let You lead. Though I can't always anticipate the movements, I know You are a good leader. I can trust where You lead me, knowing You have the big picture in mind. I pray You would make my life a beautiful dance.

Change the Way You Think

The attitude of the dance doesn't just apply to our walk with God. It also applies to the things we create.

Great work—work that impacts others—is dynamic. It requires a push and a pull. It can't always be made in neat, straight lines. It needs to adapt to the music—to the world and the lives around us.

I encourage you to create like you're dancing. Be willing to adjust at a moment's notice. Don't be afraid to get out of control. Let the world swirl around you and relax. Enjoy it. Create in the dance.

Challenge

Create something inspired by the passage in Zephaniah 3:17—"For the Lord your God is living among you. He is a mighty savior. He will take delight in you with gladness. With his love, he will calm all your fears. He will rejoice over you with joyful songs."

Especially focus on that last sentence. In the original Hebrew, the word *rejoice* is translated more literally as spinning around under violent emotion. So look at that last sentence as—He spins around under violent emotion—dancing over you with joyful songs.

Through your preferred medium, create something that captures the essence of that passage. If it's dance, what would that verse look like as a dance? If it's paint, what would that scene look like? If it's music, what song would God be dancing to?

BE INTENTIONAL

> *Find the balance between following traditions and living intentionally, purposefully.*

Spiritual Development

Let me go over with you again exactly what goes on in the Lord's Supper and why it is so centrally important. I received my instructions from the Master himself and passed them on to you. The Master, Jesus, on the night of his betrayal, took bread. Having given thanks, he broke it and said,

This is my body, broken for you.

Do this to remember me.

After supper, he did the same thing with the cup:

This cup is my blood, my new covenant with you.

Each time you drink this cup, remember me.

What you must solemnly realize is that every time you eat this bread and every time you drink this cup, you reenact in your words and actions the death of the Master. You will be drawn back to this meal again and again until the Master returns. You must never let familiarity breed contempt.

1 CORINTHIANS 11:23–26 (MSG)

THE MOST FULFILLING LIFE is the one lived intentionally. Intentionality means understanding why we do what we do.

The Lord's Supper is such an important tradition in the church. It's one of the few traditional elements actually commanded in Scriptures. And it's a great tradition.

Unfortunately, traditions can easily lose their meaning. Why do we pray before we eat? Why do we get baptized? Why do we celebrate the Lord's Supper? So often traditions in our lives devolve to meaningless activities when we forget the reason the tradition exists. The reason for the Lord's Supper is pretty simply laid out: "Do this to remember me." The whole point of the tradition is to point back to God.

Every tradition exists to point back to God. This applies to every aspect of our lives—even things that aren't traditions. Everything should ultimately point back to God. That is the sole purpose of our lives.

It's too easy to live life on autopilot. There are so many things we need to do in our lives. Work, pay bills, exercise, eat . . . it's easy to get wrapped up in these daily occurrences. But life is about remembering and pointing to God. Everything you do should be in remembrance of Him. As 1 Corinthians 10:31 (NIV) says, "whether you eat or drink or whatever you do, do it all for the glory of God."

That's what it takes to live intentionally. It requires attaching purpose to every one of our activities.

When we don't live life intentionally, it's very easy to let familiarity breed contempt. We can start hating our job, our mortgage, our possessions, our traditions . . .

Perhaps you've already felt the contempt of life—living without intentionality. It's time to remember the purpose of your life: to bring glory to God and to point to Him. God created us in His image. When we "image" something, we mirror it, reflect it, resemble it. To mirror God, behaving like

Him, is to worship Him. Being made in God's image means we were created for worship.

Perhaps you haven't yet felt contempt for life. Don't let that happen to you. Live intentionally. Live your life to remember God.

Prayer Starter

God, help me to live intentionally. I know that everything I do is meant to remember You. I choose, no matter what I do, to do it all for Your glory. Help me remember my purpose and the call You have on my life.

Change the Way You Think

Let's apply this concept to our work.

A tradition—rules and frameworks—isn't a bad thing. It exists for a purpose. The trap comes when we forget the purpose of those rules and frameworks.

When an artist forgets why rules and frameworks are there, art quickly becomes formulaic. Conversely, when artists throw out all rules and frameworks, their art becomes confusing and sloppy.

We have to understand why the rules are there so we know when we can throw them out. You might find some rules/frameworks that apply to other projects don't apply to yours; you might find some that do.

Don't be afraid of traditions. But don't be bound by them. Understand them and remember why they're there.

Challenge

Find an artistic medium that's least like your usual medium. Then find a book that discusses the rules and frameworks of that discipline. Look for ways to incorporate those into your work.

Be sure to explore why they exist and what benefit they'll bring to your project. The idea isn't to hinder the creative process, but rather to help you create with intentionality.

BE CURIOUS

> *Curiosity killed the cat.*
> *But it's worth the risk.*

Spiritual Development

It is the glory of God to conceal a thing; but the glory of kings is to search out a matter.

PROVERBS 25:2 (ASV)

I'M FASCINATED BY OLIVES. They're such an important fruit in the Bible and in all of history. The tree's wood, the fruit's oil . . . all very important. But did you know the olive by itself is extremely bitter? It's unpalatable.

It's only through the fermenting and curing of the olive that it becomes the tasty treat so many enjoy today.

Who was the first person to eat a raw olive, then experiment with it to discover how it could taste good? How did he decide to rinse the fruit excessively, then stick it in salt water for a couple days?

It had to be someone very curious.

Look at the earlier passage. I love it. It almost shows a hide-and-seek playing God. He delights in hiding things for us to discover. God wants us to be curious.

He created an enormous universe for us to explore. Then He gave us the intellect and resources to do just that! We'll never fully understand the universe. We aren't even close to understanding our own planet—the depths of the sea, the makeup of our core.

This tells me one big thing about God: He isn't threatened by our questions. He wants us to explore and ponder—to challenge and question.

Christianity isn't meant to be a blind faith. Obviously we will never have all the answers—just like science will never have all the answers. But we also shouldn't be afraid to delve into and test our faith. It does hold up to God-fearing scrutiny.

The world needs more curious Christians—Christians willing to explore their faith. We need to be delving into the mysteries of God and His Word. There's more than just history and pithy proverbs inside. There are stories and mysteries that rival J. J. Abrams's greatest masterpiece.

So I encourage you. Be curious about your faith.

Prayer Starter

I'm so glad I don't have to check my brain at the door when it comes to my faith. Thank You, God, that You aren't threatened when I ask questions and search for You. I pray that You'd put a God-fearing curiosity in me that searches out the matters You've concealed for Your own glory. Help me to have faith in You when those matters are beyond my comprehension.

Change the Way You Think

They say curiosity killed the cat. I say it's worth the risk. Just like the world needs curious Christians, the world needs curious artists.

Curiosity is necessary to the creative process. It's the voice that asks, "What if?" It's the voice that helped humanity build the first airplane, discover electricity, and brew our first cup of coffee. "What if" is very necessary.

Too often, the "what if" attitude is considered inefficient and impractical. Teachers, loan officers afraid of new business methods, and even parents can discourage you from curiosity.

Unlearn those bad habits. Renew and foster that curiosity inside you. It will make your work better and will ultimately lead to a better world. Let's be a world full of the curious!

Challenge

Come up with a really bad idea. Then start exploring at least three ways that bad idea could actually be a good idea. This will help develop your "what if" impulse. (You might want to use the appendix at the end of this book for ideas.)

Example: Speed limit signs that change the speed limit randomly. How that could be good:

1. They could adjust themselves to driving patterns. They could raise the limit for slow drivers and lower the limit for fast drivers. It would make everyone drive the same.

2. They could change depending on the time of day.

3. People would pay more attention to the signs.

This is a silly exercise, but it will get your curiosity flowing. Once you're done with the exercise, don't stop there. Keep that curiosity flowing through all your projects.

BE TENACIOUS

> *It's through wrestling
> and perseverance that we
> create great work.*

Spiritual Development

But Jacob stayed behind by himself, and a man wrestled with him until daybreak. When the man saw that he couldn't get the best of Jacob as they wrestled, he deliberately threw Jacob's hip out of joint.

The man said, "Let me go; it's daybreak."

Jacob said, "I'm not letting you go 'til you bless me."

The man said, "What's your name?"

He answered, "Jacob."

The man said, "But no longer. Your name is no longer Jacob. From now on it's Israel (God-Wrestler); you've wrestled with God and you've come through."

GENESIS 32:24–28 (MSG)

THIS IS SUCH AN interesting passage in the Bible. It seems so random. Jacob is concerned that his brother is about to sweep in and attack all his family and wealth. So he makes preparations to ensure their safety, then goes off on his own.

And while on his own, he gets in a skirmish with someone—a wrestling match. WWE Raw had nothing on this match. A man's hip got dislocated. Nothing fake here. Not only that, it turns out the villain in this story is the hero, and He is God!

It's a great story with a surprise ending. What stands out the most is Jacob's persistence. God dislocates Jacob's hip, but still Jacob won't let go. Jacob was tenacious.

Jacob knew this man had the power to do good things for him. I believe he had an idea it was God. He decided to hold on to God through the pain. He chose the blessing of God over convenience. It turns out the broken hip was a test and a blessing. Jacob passed it and received it. He didn't cut and run.

How many of us can say we have the persistence of Jacob? Would we have the resolve to stick it out with God, even when it feels like He dislocated our hip?

There are times in life when it seems God is trying to escape or trying to hurt us. Those are the times to hold on tightest. Those are the times to persevere. Because through wrestling with God, He blesses us—if we don't give up. Never give up on God. He'll never give up on you.

Prayer Starter

God, teach me the beauty of perseverance. I pray I'd have the resolve to never let go of You—even when times are tough and it feels like You're trying to escape or hurt me. Give me patience to endure the mean times as I wait for the blessing You have for me.

Change the Way You Think

Your work is a similar wrestling match. There are creative blocks, scarce resources, and our own insecurities that act as opponents in a fight. It seems like they want to defeat you—to hurt you.

Let me encourage you. In the same way we persevere with God, we never give up in the wrestle with the things we create. It's through the wrestling and the perseverance that we create great work. Just like gold and silver get refined through heat, our creations are refined through the wrestling match.

When we can push through the insecurities, resource boundaries, and creative blocks, the resulting production is that much richer. Don't give up. The result is worth the struggle.

Challenge

Choose a problem that's impossible to solve. Choose something like world hunger, the water crisis in Africa, or corruption in foreign governments. Wrestle with that. Let it break your heart a bit.

As you wrestle, look for creative solutions. You don't have to go through the local governments. You don't have to employ the United Nations. Create a list. Look for truly unique ways to combat those real issues.

If you find some ways that would really work, start a movement. But even if you don't, you can apply that thought process to your projects and your work. Let that wrestling carry over to everything you do.

of hu
ng ue
s. He
think
and

BE REDEMPTIVE

> *Great art is honest. The*
> *greatest art is redemptive.*

Spiritual Development

Look at these wicked people—enjoying a life of ease while their riches multiply. Did I keep my heart pure for nothing? Did I keep myself innocent for no reason? I get nothing but trouble all day long; every morning brings me pain. If I had really spoken this way to others, I would have been a traitor to your people. So I tried to understand why the wicked prosper. But what a difficult task it is!

. . .

Then I realized that my heart was bitter, and I was all torn up inside. I was so foolish and ignorant—I must have seemed like a senseless animal to you. Yet I still belong to you; you hold my right hand.

PSALM 73:12–16, 21–23

I LOVE THE BRUTAL honesty of this psalm. There are times when Asaph is accusing God. He's frustrated, and he can't understand why God would let the wicked prosper when he is having a rough time.

I think most of us can relate to Asaph's confusion and frustration with God. He just doesn't do things the way we think He should! It's enough to make you pray some PG-13 expressions to God.

I love the fact that folks like Asaph, David, Moses, and Paul prayed some very honest PG-13—and even R-rated— prayers. They prayed some things that would make the deacons' wives blush—not safe for church.

But God isn't threatened by our passionate prayers. He really wants us to be honest—inside and out (See Psalm 51:6). We can bring Him our frustrations, our hurts, and even our accusations. He isn't afraid of our questions, and He doesn't blush when we bring them to Him. We can be open with Him, and He won't leave us wanting.

As Asaph brought his accusations to God, God began to work on Asaph's heart. It probably wasn't an instantaneous revelation. Eventually Asaph saw that his accusations against God weren't merited. His heart was softened toward God, and he got a clearer picture of reality. God is in control.

And God didn't reject Asaph for his honesty. He still belonged to God. God still held him with His right hand.

God won't reject you for your honesty. He wants it from you. He also wants to take you beyond your honesty—to redemption.

Prayer Starter

God, there are times I don't understand Your plan. Sometimes I get frustrated or angry with You. I pray You would open my eyes to see Your goodness and show me that You desire truth from me. You desire an honest relationship. You also want to bring me past my hurts to a place where my perspective is clearer. Help me to see Your perspective.

Change the Way You Think

Honesty is a vital part of creativity. Great art is honest art. Paintings of rainbows and puppy dogs wear thin when you aren't always feeling rainbow and puppy-dog feelings. A great artist will paint it all, even the darker parts within.

It's also important to realize that, as believers, we have a hope beyond the darkness and pain. We don't have to drag our work through the mud and leave it there.

There is a glorious end to the pain we experience. As Proverbs 4:18 says, "The way of the righteous is like the first gleam of dawn, which shines ever brighter until the full light of day."

We can bring that same hope and that same redemption to our work. Great art is honest. The greatest art is redemptive.

Challenge

Think back to a painful moment in your career. Perhaps it was embarrassing or involved betrayal—maybe something quite ugly. Now start to wrestle with that moment. Don't let it become the victor. Look for the beauty hidden in that moment. In every bit of pain is beauty.

Now use the beauty of that ugly moment to create something. Use your particular medium of creation and capture the beauty from that moment. We are representatives of God's work on the earth. And part of His work is making beauty from ashes.

BE INVESTED

> *It's not good for man
> to create alone.*

Spiritual Development

I turned my head and saw yet another wisp of smoke on its way to nothingness: a solitary person, completely alone—no children, no family, no friends—yet working obsessively late into the night, compulsively greedy for more and more, never bothering to ask, "Why am I working like a dog, never having any fun? And who cares?" More smoke. A bad business.

It's better to have a partner than go it alone. Share the work, share the wealth. And if one falls down, the other helps, But if there's no one to help, tough!

. . .

By yourself you're unprotected. With a friend you can face the worst. Can you round up a third? A three-stranded rope isn't easily snapped.

ECCLESIASTES 4:7–10,12 (MSG)

MY WIFE AND I discovered the power of community the difficult way. We had just moved away from our family—her to start a new school and me to become a full-time writer. We were in a new city with no friends.

So we both committed ourselves wholly to our respective work. We were the ones working obsessively into the night trying to conquer our mountains—until we had to stop.

Our health began deteriorating. We weren't sleeping. Anxiety. Depression. We had nothing to distract us from our work and work was our lives. Even our relationships with God began to suffer.

That's not the way to live. We quickly learned we needed friends.

God didn't create us to be alone. That was the first thing He saw in His creation that wasn't good—that man was alone. The creation of woman was the solution to the problem.

But we see it's also not just about two—they were called to multiply. More people. The idea is community. The right kind of community is a group that supports each other and points each other toward the right things. It's vital.

Do you have a community that helps you keep things in perspective? Do they encourage you in the things of God? Do they tell you to put down your respective paint and canvas and have a little fun?

You aren't living in the stride God created for you if you don't. I encourage you: embrace community in your life. Get involved volunteering at your church. Join Bible studies. Reach out to the right people. Invest in them and let them invest back in you.

Prayer Starter

God, show me the power of community. Give me friends that will support me when I fall. Surround me with those that will point me toward You and keep my perspective correct. I don't want to be the solitary person—completely alone. I want to be part of a healthy community.

Change the Way You Think

Artists are notorious for being loners. We are the ones working obsessively late into the night. Though we may not be greedy for money (starving artist, anyone?), we are greedy for self-esteem and affirmation.

When we get that affirmation, it's a brief respite to our desire for more. But we are never truly satisfied. That's not what satisfies.

Community does satisfy. It helps to brainstorm and share your ideas with folks.

But more than that, a good community will help you when you reach those doldrums of despair. We all go through them. You aren't alone in that. And it's much better to go through those valley times with others who have been there than to trudge through them alone.

Challenge

Find a creative friend for this task. Find them on social media or in person. Switch projects with them. Give them the vision for your particular project, and take their vision for their project. (Choose a small pet project to reduce the risk, or go risky and give them something important.)

This exercise will open the lines of communication between you and a different perspective. It will get you outside of yourself and help you see from another person's perspective. Learn from the experience.

BE RESISTED

The greatest minds in our world have met the same resistance you have. Let it fuel you onward.

Spiritual Development

Then Jesus told them, "A prophet is honored everywhere except in his own hometown and among his relatives and his own family." And because of their unbelief, he couldn't do any miracles among them except to place his hands on a few sick people and heal them.

MARK 6:4–5

In an interview on *The Daily Show with Jon Stewart*, on November 18, 2011, Martin Scorcese discussed a conversation he had with his daughter. She told him (in reference to making a movie), "You should find what people like and make a movie about that." Obviously, Little Scorcese isn't a fan of her father's movies. A prophet is not honored in his own hometown.

This can be a source of much frustration, especially for someone like me. I crave admiration, but I often don't get it from the places I want it most. It's easy as an artist to assume my friends and family don't appreciate me. It's easy to disconnect and get frustrated. Do you relate?

Some people even get resentful. Some hop from project to project seeking new appreciation. We become like appreciation junkies—jonesing for our next fix. Each new project offers a temporary high, but it eventually wears off as you become the resident hometown prophet.

Check your attitude if you're experiencing this phenomena on a sustained basis. It's natural to seek approval, but our self-worth should not come from our surroundings. It should ultimately come from Above.

Jesus wasn't respected in His hometown. But He didn't stop doing good works. His call and affirmation came from Higher. Your call comes from Higher. Live to bring honor and glory to God.

The only affirmation that truly matters will come in eternity, when God tells us, "Well done, good and faithful servant! You have been faithful with a few things; I will put you in charge of many things. Come and share your master's happiness!" (Matt. 25:21 NIV)

Prayer Starter

I choose to look to You for affirmation, Heavenly Father—not the people that surround me. I want to follow the example of Jesus. I want to keep persevering in good works regardless of whether or not it's appreciated. As Galatians 6:9 encourages me, I will not lose heart in doing good, for in due time I will reap if I don't grow weary.

Change the Way You Think

Yes, if we are constantly seeking people's approval, we will be consistently let down.

But people's approval is never an indication that we are doing something worthwhile. Mankind's greatest endeavors have all met not only indifference and disrespect but also strong opposition. Any time we choose to break the status quo, we will meet resistance.

I worry when I'm not met with resistance. Resistance is often the litmus test that you're doing something that will break the status quo.

The world needs the status quo broken. As long as there's poverty and pain—which is the default state of the world—we need things to change. We need new ideas to solve these problems. That's the beauty of creativity—it's the surest vehicle for overthrowing the status quo.

So don't be discouraged when you experience the hometown prophet syndrome. Embrace it as a challenge. The greatest minds in our world have met the same resistance. Let it fuel you onward.

Challenge

Look for an overused or outdated technique from your area of work. Feel free to reach back ten or twenty years to something that's currently laughed about or forgotten.

Now take that technique and adopt it—at least for one project. Turn that outdated technique and make it fresh and unique. Use it in a way no one else has thought to use it. Make it your own. Push through the internal and external resistance.

(If you need an example, I designed a logo for my online magazine as an animated GIF—a mockable technology. I've kept it and I love it.)

BE LIBERAL

Inspiration isn't in short supply. Don't hold it back.

Spiritual Development

Whatever is good and perfect comes down to us from God our Father, who created all the lights in the heavens. He never changes or casts a shifting shadow. He chose to give birth to us by giving us his true word. And we, out of all creation, became his prized possession.

JAMES 1:17–18

I HAVE A CAR. I can walk. I have a lovely wife. I eat three square meals a day.

I don't mean to brag, but I have it pretty good.

But there are times I feel like a waste of blessing. There are times I don't appreciate what I have. Why would God possibly waste such amazing things on someone who doesn't even appreciate or recognize the blessing?

Because God's awesome. That's not a trite saying. He's so good to us.

The coolest thing about His goodness is that it doesn't end. It's not some limited resource like money or gasoline. He doesn't have to hold back because it doesn't run out. When He blesses me, it doesn't keep Him from blessing someone else.

It's important that we get the correct perspective on God. He is a good God. So many times we focus on troubles and trials in our lives and lose sight of that He is good. We focus on the negative 1 percent of our lives and miss out on the amazing 99 percent.

When we live in that tiny 1 percent, we have small lives. We focus inward. We lose sight of the beauty around us. We aren't meant to live in that small box. We're meant to live in the 99 percent.

As Paul tells us in 1 Thessalonians 5:18, "Be thankful in all circumstances, for this is God's will for you who belong to Christ Jesus."

Prayer Starter

God, help me learn to be thankful in all circumstances. I don't want to be a waste of blessing. Help me focus on the many great things You've given me instead of focusing on the small. I want to live a grateful life that honors You.

Change the Way You Think

Just like God has an endless supply of blessings, He's given us an endless supply of creativity. Seriously.

James 1:5 tells us that if we need wisdom, God gives it to us liberally. Wisdom is simply a form of creativity. It's seeing the world through the right perspective to inform your decisions.

So creativity isn't a scarce resource.

That means you don't have to hold back your very best. You don't have to save some of your ideas for your next project. You can pour yourself into your work—knowing the ideas will be there for the next one. And the next . . .

I've found my greatest creative blocks come when I try to hoard ideas. When I hold onto ideas and keep them to myself, they crowd the creative space in my brain. But when I prime the creativity pump of my brain by releasing my ideas, new ones start flowing.

Challenge

Do an idea dump. List all your best ideas in a Word document or in a Moleskin, then start fresh. You can come back to the ideas later. But for today's projects, ignore every one of your ideas/techniques you listed.

This creative challenge might give you indigestion or make your palms sweaty, but that's good. A little discomfort will spark some unique thoughts.

BE BRAVE

> *Fearing people is a*
> *dangerous trap—devoid*
> *of creative power.*

Spiritual Development

**Fearing people is a dangerous trap, but trusting the
Lord means safety.**

PROVERBS 29:25

ANTHROPOPHOBIA IS THE FEAR of people. That's not the fear
Proverbs is talking about, though. It isn't a form of social
anxiety disorder or some fear of germs. What Proverbs is
talking about is more like allodoxaphobia.

Allodoxaphobia is the fear of other people's opinions. I'm
pretty sure almost everyone who produces something has an
undiagnosed case of this phobia. We are all desperately insecure and fear what others think about us and our work.

Sometimes it can keep us from even trying or from making our work public. We don't want to risk the negative opinions people might have.

Proverbs says this is a trap.

No matter what we do in life, we'll never be able to avoid negative opinions. It just isn't possible. In fact, there are even times when doing the right thing will make you look worse than if you had done the wrong thing. We've all heard the stories of corporate whistle-blowers losing jobs and pensions for doing the right thing.

It can be discouraging, seeing bad people get ahead while good people get in trouble. It's enough to make you want to write an angry psalm or two! (See Psalm 73).

But we can't fall into the trap of living for what people think. We need to live lives of integrity, regardless of how it looks to those around us. We need to trust and fear the Lord. That's where true safety lies.

Prayer Starter

God, I want to honor You by trusting in You. Forgive me for living to please those around me. I pray You give me the courage to do what's right no matter how I may appear to others.

Change the Way You Think

That same fear of people leads us to be bashful when we share ourselves with others. We fear rejection if our work isn't perfect or accepted by the masses. So we shrink into our dark corners and hide our creativity. We keep it secret in our journals or closets—tinkering here and there. We're trying to perfect it. But even when it's right, we fear showing it to others. "What if they judge me?"

Let me tell you a secret: everyone in this world is desperately insecure. We all have those fears—fears of what others will think of us. Regardless of how far along you are in your craft, you'll deal with this fear.

The people that succeed in life put it to the side and create in spite of it. They put themselves out there and risk rejection. Trust me. It's a risk worth taking.

Challenge

Work on something publicly. Start a new project and do it where everyone can see you. If you're painting, sit down on a busy street corner and do it there. If you're choreographing a dance, do it in a park. If you're designing a graphic on your computer, live stream the screen capture to friends or anyone else who wants to see.

This exercise will expose your good ideas as well as your bad ideas. You might feel like a failure when people see your ideas that didn't work out—but you aren't. We all have a thousand bad ideas before we get a good idea. This exercise will help you get over your fear by facing it head on.

BE DUAL

> *A successful life is breaking the rules just as much as following them.*

Spiritual Development

For when I tried to keep the law, it condemned me. So I died to the law—I stopped trying to meet all its requirements—so that I might live for God. My old self has been crucified with Christ. It is no longer I who live, but Christ lives in me. So I live in this earthly body by trusting in the Son of God, who loved me and gave himself for me.

GALATIANS 2:19–20

I LOVE THIS SEEMINGLY contradictory paragraph. In two sentences, Paul says he's both dead *and* alive. Christ lives *His* life in Paul, yet Paul also lives his *own* life. When Paul tells us in Galatians that we have died to the law, it's impossible for us to wrap our minds around it. When we choose to die to sin and the law, we open ourselves up to live for God.

The Bible is filled with these paradoxes.

1. God is three people, but He is also One. (Matt. 28:19 and Deut. 6:4)

2. The greatest person is the one who serves others. (Matt. 23:11)

3. Whoever loses his life will find it. (Matt. 10:39)

It would be easy to think these thoughts are contradictory. However, you don't understand the whole truth about God until you can believe both of them. God's truth is greater than our ability to perceive. He wants us to explore that truth.

I love how The Message paraphrases Proverbs 25:2–3: "God delights in concealing things; scientists delight in discovering things. Like the horizons for breadth and the ocean for depth, the understanding of a good leader is broad and deep."

God is a great leader. And just like we couldn't possibly grasp the horizon or comprehend the depths of the oceans, we'll never completely understand the fullness of God. That doesn't mean we shouldn't try.

Christians are often criticized for having blind faith—ignoring reality and choosing to believe a fictitious story. I believe we get that bad rap because we don't search. We believe something at face value without searching into the matter. It's the glory of peasants to eat what's spoon-fed to them, but it's the glory of kings to delve into a matter and explore.

Let's be kingly Christians. Let's search into the seemingly impossible matters of the Bible and come out with a deeper understanding of who God is.

Prayer Starter

God, I know it's impossible to fully grasp the truth about You. That doesn't mean I don't want to try. I pray that You would reveal Yourself to me and open my eyes to even greater mysteries. Let my faith be real but not blind—knowing You are the deepest mystery and the greatest thing worth exploring.

Change the Way You Think

It's the human condition to simplify the world until all mystery is gone. Ever since we ate from the Tree of the Knowledge of Good and Evil, we've taken it upon ourselves to categorize the world and remove all mystery. We wanted to know the difference between good and evil for ourselves. We wanted black and white. So we started creating and adhering strictly to countless rules and formulas. That ultimately limits our creativity.

On the other hand, rules or formulas are there because they work. We've discovered what's aesthetically pleasing, so we turn it into a rule. We analyze successful businesses and find things they have in common. In doing so, we avoid common pitfalls.

At the same time, the rule isn't all there is. Adhering to rules and formulas doesn't make you successful. Neither does ignoring the rules completely.

As creative people, we need to learn submissive rebellion. We need to study the rules and learn the formulas. However, we also need to break the rules and, from time to time, do it intentionally. We need to choose carefully the rule we'll break and do it purposefully. While rules can be true, they are not conclusive.

The truth of God, creativity personified, is filled with seeming paradoxes. Why wouldn't the essence of His nature be the same? We need to be willing to embrace the creative paradox to tap into the fullness of possibilities.

"The test of a first-rate intelligence is the ability to hold two opposed ideas in the mind at the same time, and still retain the ability to function."[1]

Challenge

Intentionally break rules today. Pick a project—pet project or real project—and choose a rule or rules you want to break. Be intentional about it. Find a way to create a masterpiece in spite of established rules. You might discover a new rule that comes alongside the old one. You might fail miserably.

Open yourself up to the idea that rules are essential but at the same time flexible.

BE PREPARED

Seek inspiration when you don't need it, so it's there when you do.

Spiritual Development

You lazy fool, look at an ant.
  Watch it closely; let it teach you a thing or two.
  Nobody has to tell it what to do.
  All summer it stores up food; at harvest it stockpiles provisions.
  So how long are you going to laze around doing nothing?
  How long before you get out of bed?
  A nap here, a nap there, a day off here, a day off there,
  sit back, take it easy—do you know what comes next?
  Just this: You can look forward to a dirt-poor life,
  poverty your permanent houseguest!

PROVERBS 6:6–11 (MSG)

THIS VERSE MIGHT BE a bit harsh, but it's an important principle—preparing for hard times. In the good seasons of our lives it's easy to sit back and enjoy it. We should enjoy it. We shouldn't, however, allow the good times to make us lazy.

The good seasons in our lives are when we need to begin investing for the bad seasons. And this is true for more than just finances or food items. It's true relationally too.

Marriages and families aren't lost in the bad times. They're lost in the good times. When things are going well, it's too easy to neglect investing in the relationships. When you and your spouse aren't arguing, it's easy to ignore them. But those are the times you need to invest love and respect in your spouse. That builds up a storage of good will. So when the arguments or rough times come, you have a bank account of appreciation and love to draw from.

Our ability to invest in relationships in the good times determines how the bad times will go. The same is true with friendships, children, employee/employer relationships . . . and more importantly, our relationship with God.

When we make it a priority to chat with God and study His Word in the good times, when the bad times come we have provisions to survive the storm. When things don't work out like we wanted them to—when a loved one dies, when we lose our job—we aren't so quick to blame God, and we have the resources to fight our pain and discouragement. Our relationship remains strong because we invested in it during the good times.

This doesn't mean bad times are a breeze. Yet we handle them in much more constructive ways when we prepare during the good times.

Prayer Starter

God, I want to learn the lesson You've taught me through the illustration of the ant. I want to store up provisions during the good times. I want to invest in my relationships with family, friends, and especially You. Help me see opportunities to stockpile my love in the good times. Help me draw from that love during the bad times and draw closer to You and to those that are important in my life.

Change the Way You Think

Just like it's important to store up financial provisions, it's important to store up creative provisions. If you're in a particularly motivated season of your life right now, you need to capture every idea. You need to find a way to store that inspiration. Carry around a recorder, a notebook, a camera. Find every way to capture inspiration for the dry times of your life.

Blaine Hogan refers to it as "scratching when you don't itch" in his book *Untitled: Thoughts on the Creative Process*. It's looking for chances to get inspired even when you don't need it. It's keeping track of great ideas even when you're not looking for them.

Ants may not be particularly creative. But we can learn a thing or two about creativity from them.

Challenge

Come up with ten projects or ideas you'll probably never attempt. Write them down. Now list ideas that will make those projects a success. Come up with two or three creative ideas that would make those projects unique.

Save that list. The project list will probably never be valuable to you. But the ideas that make those projects a success will apply to future projects. And though they may seem unrelated, you'll be able to reuse those ideas for future projects.

BE FRESH

*Great work is less about new-
ness, more about freshness.*

Spiritual Development

**What do people get for all their hard work under the
sun? Generations come and generations go, but the
earth never changes.**

. . .

**Everything is wearisome beyond description. No
matter how much we see, we are never satisfied. No
matter how much we hear, we are not content. History merely repeats itself. It has all been done before. Nothing under the sun is truly new. Sometimes
people say, "Here is something new!" But actually it
is old; nothing is ever truly new. We don't remember
what happened in the past, and in future generations, no one will remember what we are doing now.**

ECCLESIASTES 1:3–4, 8–11

KING SOLOMON WROTE THOSE words during a dark period of
his life. It sounds like something I would write in a journal—
during one of my depressed moods after a failure or a rough
couple of weeks.

While this passage is extremely depressing, it's also true . . . at least partly. There's nothing new and everything is wearisome beyond description—under the sun. The phrase "under the sun," speaks of everything humanity has to offer: wisdom, strength, creativity, ambition. It's ultimately all meaningless.

We will never be satisfied; we will never create anything new when it comes from our earthly powers.

The only things that truly satisfy are eternal. Our love for and relationship with God is the most important thing in our lives. As we examined on Day 4, that's the reason we were put on this earth: to glorify God and to enjoy Him forever.[2]

It's so easy to forget that. It's easy to get distracted and think that life is all about the rat race. We wear ourselves out working too hard—all to satisfy our insatiable, vain ambitions. We spend each waking moment in survival mode. We don't stop to think, "Am I enjoying God? Am I glorifying Him by running around so much?"

When you find yourself in the pits of despair, writing words like the pitiful King Solomon, ask yourself those questions. Instead of giving into depression, refocus yourself. Rest in loving God. Take a deep breath and talk to God.

Prayer Starter

God, remind me of my true purpose. I don't want to wear myself out doing good things—even if they're in Your name. Teach me to rest in You. Teach me how to glorify You and enjoy You forever. I know, under the sun, everything is meaningless. But above the sun there is life, hope, and purpose.

Change the Way You Think

Though Solomon's musings are depressing, they're also liberating for us. So often we get caught up in the pursuit of being completely unique. We want our work to be unlike anything the world has ever seen. We get easily frustrated when it seems like everything we make is merely a remix of something that came before.

We don't have to stress about it. Yes, it's all been done before. Every bit of creative work is a combination of experiences and inspirations that already existed before. Nothing will ever be brand-new.

So relax. Take a deep breath. Take the weight of newness off your shoulders. You don't need to carry that burden. It will never happen. It's okay.

Here's the encouraging part. Your work will be unique because it comes from you. Nobody has your perspective. That's what makes a work fresh. It's the "you" that you put inside it.

The familiar helps people process your work. It helps them relate to it. If the things you produce were outrageously new, people wouldn't know what to do with them. There needs to be an element that's relatable so people can appreciate it. The new perspective you bring makes it fresh.

Your work will be fresh. Maybe not new. But fresh.

Challenge

Go on Wikipedia. Find your favorite artist's page. Skim through it. Find an interesting link in the text and click on that. Read through that entry. Find another link and click through. Repeat this about ten to fifteen times. Keep track of the various pages you've visited—your Wikipedia journey.

Each new idea builds on previous ideas. You might find that it only takes a few clicks to get from Galileo to Barney the Dinosaur. You'll also find some unique ideas you've never heard of before. Let those inspire you in your work today.

BE RELAXED

> *The sigh of relief doesn't have to come after the deadline when you turn the project in. It can come the day before.*

Spiritual Development

Heaven and Earth were finished, down to the last detail. By the seventh day God had finished his work. On the seventh day he rested from all his work. God blessed the seventh day. He made it a Holy Day because on that day he rested from his work, all the creating God had done.

GENESIS 2:1–3 (MSG)

I'M A DRIVEN INDIVIDUAL. I'm willing to bet, if you're reading this book, you are too. Driven individuals are the ones that get things done—that make the world efficient and productive. Unfortunately, they also tend to be the ones who neglect their family, their sanity, and their physical health.

God's a driven being. He's so driven, He literally makes the world go 'round. But in His ultimate act of creation, He chose to rest. It's as if God dusted off His pants, grabbed an ice-cold Dr. Pepper, and sat on His porch swing—admiring His beautiful artwork. It was good.

And He made us to function best when we follow His example of rest. He made us to have a Sabbath day—a day of rest.

Isaiah 56:2 (CEB) says, "Happy is the one who does this, the person who holds it fast, who keeps the Sabbath, not making it impure, and avoids doing any evil."

It's so popular in our culture to be a workaholic. We feel important being the first ones to arrive and the last ones to leave work. Consequently, we reorient our lives around work and productivity. We neglect more important things in our lives. That sort of thinking is toxic—it's evil. It puts all the glory of our successes on our own shoulders. God gets no glory in that. And it doesn't mean we're working harder than those who take a weekly rest. It means we're doing more than we should—or we're doing the wrong things.

When we choose to keep that Sabbath day holy, we find ourselves happy—yes, happy. God promises it. And He isn't a liar.

So I encourage you, give yourself a Sabbath day of rest. I used to work at a church; that meant Saturdays and Sundays couldn't be my Sabbath days. I took off Fridays. My pastor took off Mondays. Whatever day you choose, give that time to God, to your family, and to your sanity. Relax. Put some of the weight of success back on God's shoulders where He can get the glory.

Prayer Starter

God, teach me to keep the Sabbath day holy. Teach me to relax and trust in You, even when my body fidgets thinking of what could be accomplished if I went back to work. I know

You created the seventh day as a gift to me, and I want to honor that gift. Help me rest in You.

Change the Way You Think

Here's the most fun part of the creation story.

God's an excellent planner. He knew His deadline ahead of time. He chose a week to create everything we see. Sometimes I feel my deadlines seem just as daunting.

Even though He knew He had seven days to knock this thing out, He chose to finish it in six. He didn't work until the deadline.

Deadline. Think of that word. Death. We should not be flirting with death on every project. That's a morbid and stressful way to live.

Sometimes we need to finish before our deadlines and rest. Work hard for six proverbial days, then rest on the seventh. Give yourself a break. Don't keep tinkering and tweaking. Once you finish on that sixth day, leave it alone. Hands off. Grab a Dr. Pepper and sit on your porch swing. Enjoy the creation.

Challenge

Pick a project with a short deadline—the one that's stressing you out. Now shorten that deadline by at least one-seventh. Cut it in half if you want. Now get it done within that time frame.

Two things will come from that. First, you'll cut unnecessary elements from the project. It will help you prioritize properly. Second, it'll show you how productive you can truly be. You'd be amazed what we accomplish when we take a proper rest like God designed us to.

BE CONTENT

> *It is possible to balance personal contentment with artistic discontent.*

Spiritual Development

Actually, I don't have a sense of needing anything personally. I've learned by now to be quite content whatever my circumstances. I'm just as happy with little as with much, with much as with little. I've found the recipe for being happy whether full or hungry, hands full or hands empty. Whatever I have, wherever I am, I can make it through anything in the One who makes me who I am.

PHILIPPIANS 4:11–13 (MSG)

DO YOU REMEMBER COMPLAINING about something as a child? Maybe it was because your legs were tired while walking the mall with your parents. Remember what they said?

"You should be grateful! In my day, there was no mall. And we had no car. We had to walk fifteen miles in one day just to find a pair of shoes."

That's how our parents taught us contentment. Things could be worse. Be grateful for what you have.

When Paul's talking about contentment in the above passage, he isn't trying to shut us up by telling us things could get worse. Contentment isn't self-delusion so you can be happy even during bad situations.

Paul talks about contentment as a way to rely on God. It's an opportunity to put our trust in God. Paul experienced great riches and great poverty. He realized that those experiences of want were moments when he was forced to rely on God more deeply.

You see, anyone can praise God and say they trust Him when things are going great. But when your tummy rumbles, that's when the rubber meets the road. Do you really trust God? Are you really content in the things He's given you?

Contentment isn't tested in the good times. It's tested in the bad.

What lack do you feel today? Do you lack resources? Do you lack skills? Do you lack the connections you need?

This is your chance to rely on God to sustain you. Now is the time to put your trust in God and choose to be content whatever your circumstances.

Prayer Starter

God, teach me contentment. I want to rely on You when I have plenty and when I have nothing. Let my growling stomach remind me that I rely on You as my source—instead of an opportunity to complain. I want to rely on You in the good times and the bad times, because I know I can do everything through You who gives me strength.

Change the Way You Think

"True . . . contentment is a real, even an active virtue—
not only affirmative but creative. . . . It is the power of getting
out of any situation all there is in it."[3]

There's such an impossible balance between contentment and the desire to improve. For great work to happen,
there needs to be a certain amount of discontentment. The
discontentment can't be focused on ourselves. It must be focused externally.

Unfortunately, many artists and workers confuse discontentment with the way things are for discontentment in
themselves. We see the skills of others and feel inadequate.
We envy others' successes or achievements, wishing we had
what they had. We need to remember that we're only respon-
sible for what God has given us. That's internal contentment.

However, that doesn't mean your work doesn't need to
improve. Great work is focused externally. It's made to influence others. There has to be a discontentment. There has to
be a desire inside you to change things. We could call that an
artistic discontentment.

But the discontentment is external, not internal. That's
a difficult balance to achieve.

To be a healthy creator you have to walk that line. You
must constantly evaluate your level of personal contentment
and artistic discontentment.

Live a life of abandon to change the world. But live a life
of contentment with God.

Challenge

Choose an object in the room. Pick something that has
multiple parts (such as a chair, table, or lamp). Deconstruct
that object either physically or in your mind into individual
elements. List the different elements from that object on a

piece of paper. Resist the temptation to oversimplify. Even simple objects have their own type of complexity. There are bolts, screws, washers, stickers. . . . List them all.

Now use that list to invent. Invent some new things. Repurpose what you have into something useful, something fun, something crazy, something unique.

Invent as many things as you can using what you have. Learn to squeeze every ounce of usefulness out of the object. Appreciate the complexity of something so commonplace and ordinary.

BE GREAT

> *To do something great,
> you must give up doing
> something good.*

Spiritual Development

[F]or the light makes everything visible. This is why it is said, "Awake, O sleeper, rise up from the dead, and Christ will give you light." So be careful how you live. Don't live like fools, but like those who are wise. Make the most of every opportunity in these evil days. Don't act thoughtlessly, but understand what the Lord wants you to do.

EPHESIANS 5:14–17

I LOVE THIS QUOTE from Martin Luther (the German monk, not the junior king): "I have so much to do that if I didn't spend at least three hours a day in prayer I would never get it all done."

I don't normally think of monks as being particularly busy, but Mr. Luther was a deeply tormented and introspective man. His superior put him to work, making him super busy in an attempt to distract him from all his depressing thoughts.

So when Martin Luther says he was so busy he needed to spend three hours each day in prayer, that was saying something.

This reminds me of our verse in Ephesians. In another translation it says to redeem the time because the days are evil. That means we need to be cautious with our time. There are countless activities that pull at us. They are distractions—good things that distract us from the best things.

We have so very little time on earth. We have no business bogging ourselves down with good activities that keep us from the great activities. For instance, climbing the corporate ladder is a good thing, but developing strong family relationships is a great thing. Responding to your buddy's text is a good thing, but staring into your spouse's eyes on your date is a great thing.

I love the prayer Psalm 90:12 gives us: "Teach us to realize the brevity of life, so that we may grow in wisdom."

We need wisdom to realize what God wants us to do. Then we need the resolve to spend our time doing the great things and leaving the good things for later. There's always extra time to watch a football game or read the latest teen vampire novel. Those come after the great things.

Prayer Starter

God, teach me to realize the brevity of life so I may grow in wisdom. Help me prioritize my day to make the most of my time. Show me the things that need my attention, like my family and my relationship with You. I pray You would give me the discipline to devote my time to the best things and to not be distracted by the good things.

Change the Way You Think

Have you heard of the Pareto principle—or the 80–20 rule? It basically says that 80 percent of the results come from 20 percent of the effort.

Let's apply that to a company of one hundred people. It means 80 percent of the success of the company comes from just twenty employees. You might call those twenty the great employees. Then you could call the other eighty employees the good employees. Good employees get work done, but great employees make the company a success.

Now apply that concept to the tasks you do during the day. Eighty percent of your success comes from just 20 percent of what you do. Wouldn't it be wise to evaluate what that 20 percent is and focus on that? What if you were able to do that, then stop doing the other 80 percent of tasks?

You would have so much extra time, and you'd still be successful. Now imagine you fill your time with productive things again. You could double or even triple your productivity without ever feeling very busy.

If we apply that to the things we create, I'd like to say that 20 percent of your effort goes to the bulk of your creation. You've made a great piece of work with very little effort. But so many us then spend another 80 percent of their time perfecting our work. And it yields very little results. Imagine if you stopped at the 20 percent mark.

What more could you create? What more could you get done? Where would your work be in the next year?

Challenge

Pick your least favorite children's entertainment character. (For some, Barney immediately comes to mind.) Now focus on changing 20 percent of their identity to make them edgy. Turn them into a jail-bound rap artist or a serial killer. Keep their essence, while at the same time changing them completely. Notice how little it takes to change something so completely?

Add this to your creative journal and share it with others. See what they think.

BE PERCEPTIVE

> *Great artists help others
> see what they see.*

Spiritual Development

In the meantime, the disciples pressed him, "Rabbi, eat. Aren't you going to eat?"

He told them, "I have food to eat you know nothing about."

The disciples were puzzled. "Who could have brought him food?"

Jesus said, "The food that keeps me going is that I do the will of the One who sent me, finishing the work he started. As you look around right now, wouldn't you say that in about four months it will be time to harvest? Well, I'm telling you to open your eyes and take a good look at what's right in front of you. These Samaritan fields are ripe. It's harvest time!

JOHN 4:31–35 (MSG)

JESUS WAS ABOUT TO have a good ol' fashioned tent revival at a well. He was deeply affecting the life of a Samaritan woman, and she was out urging all the townspeople to meet this amazing guy. Life change was on the horizon.

Enter the goofy sidekicks—the disciples. This story makes them seem a bit dense. They weren't dense. They just had the wrong perspective on the situation. Jesus saw things they couldn't grasp because they hadn't trained themselves to think like He thought.

Think of an elaborate party. The room's filled with foreign dignitaries and celebrities. Now imagine a Navy Seal shows up—especially one that's just come back from a battle. Mr. Navy Seal walks into the shindig and immediately sizes it up. He's scanning the room to identify potential weapons and escape routes. He's already decided the order in which he'd kill people if something went down. Mr. Navy Seal sees things I will never see—because he's trained himself to think that way. I haven't.

That's what this story is like. Jesus was seeing things from a Navy Seal's perspective while the disciples were noticing the pretty place settings.

When we become believers, we're recruited into an elite squad. We're brought from the kingdom of darkness into the kingdom of light.

We can no longer be content to notice the elaborate place settings on the tables, knowing there's a legitimate battle raging on around us. We need to train ourselves to see the things God sees. We need to think bigger. We need to think eternally.

Romans 12:2 puts it succinctly: "Don't copy the behavior and customs of this world, but let God transform you into a new person by changing the way you think. Then you will learn to know God's will for you, which is good and pleasing and perfect."

There's something bigger going on around us—God's will. We need to train our brains to focus on that, to see that.

Prayer Starter

God, teach me to see things like You see them. I want to have a larger perspective than to just see things at face value. Teach me to see the fields are ripe. You have a will for me, and I want to act accordingly.

Change the Way You Think

Great artists train themselves to think differently too. And no, I'm not trying to promote Apple.

When a graphic designer reads a magazine, he notices layout and graphic techniques that elude me. When a skilled musician attends a concert, she hears tones and rhythms that I miss.

This sort of thing comes naturally to a skilled artist because they are obsessed with their craft. It's hard not to notice those things.

But for me to notice them, it requires a bit of training and focus. It requires me to avoid what I'd normally see—the face value—and search deeper to observe the details. Instead of just consuming a piece of art, I actively unfold and explore it.

If you want to develop as an artist, as an employee, as anything, you need to constantly train yourself to actively unfold and explore the things you see. These things can't just be a form of entertainment—it must be a journey of discovery. You must train your brain to see the world differently. You must train to be a Navy Seal in your world.

Challenge

Walk into a crowded room. Try to size it up like a jewel thief. Plan your heist. Imagine how you could break in and how you would escape. Who would you need to recruit to help you with the heist? Imagine what could go wrong and plan for contingencies.

Do *not* act on this fantasy. But train your brain to see the situation a bit differently. You'll probably run through some intriguing scenarios in your head—which is entertaining in itself. You can also start putting yourself in other roles and imagining other scenarios. Explore these scenarios and let them inspire you for the things you create.

BE PARALLEL

> *Need a breakthrough for your work? Look for a seemingly unrelated breakthrough. You'll find it there.*

Spiritual Development

His disciples came and asked him, "Why do you use parables when you talk to the people?"

He replied, "You are permitted to understand the secrets of the Kingdom of Heaven, but others are not. To those who listen to my teaching, more understanding will be given, and they will have an abundance of knowledge. But for those who are not listening, even what little understanding they have will be taken away from them. That is why I use these parables, For they look, but they don't really see. They hear, but they don't really listen or understand."

MATTHEW 13:10–13

JESUS UNFOLDS A HUGE mystery in this passage. The disciples questioned why He spoke in parables—everyday stories with parallel, spiritual meanings. Jesus basically said, "I do it to confuse people who don't really want to know the truth about God." He was trying to turn people off who came to Him with the wrong motives. Crazy, huh?

Seems like a jerk move, but then He says, "For those who do want to know, it makes it easier to understand."

Jesus realized that this whole God thing isn't an exclusively cerebral matter. It's equally a heart matter. We don't come to God, through Jesus, simply because all the facts line up. We come to Him because our hearts are softened and we want to respond to His love.

God said, "If you look for me wholeheartedly, you will find me" (Jer. 29:13).

It's exciting to know that God isn't trying to conceal the truth from us. He isn't playing a cruel game of hide-and-seek. He wants us to find Him.

We just need to approach our search with humility and sincerity.

Prayer Starter

God, reveal Yourself to me. I know You want to show me more of Your grace, mercy, and truth. Teach me to seek You with humility and sincerity. Open up new knowledge of You as I seek You with my whole heart.

Change the Way You Think

One of the coolest things about the parables is that they help us understand impossible truths. Spiritual matters aren't exactly simple. But when Jesus frames them in everyday stories, it helps us get a glimpse of a truth far beyond what we could normally grasp.

That's the power of parallel thinking. One seemingly un-related truth can help us understand another truth.

That's why so many of the nuggets in Proverbs are para-bles or comparisons. "Can a man scoop fire into his lap with-out his clothes being burned? Can a man walk on hot coals without his feet being scorched? So is he who sleeps with another man's wife; no one who touches her will go unpun-ished" (Prov. 6:27–29 NIV).

There's so much wisdom in parallel thinking. It's one of the biggest sources of creative breakthrough.

Thomas Edison, one of the world's most prolific inven-tors, constantly thought in parallel. That's how he created the phonograph and the movie reel. What one device did for your eye, the other device could do for your ear.

I want to encourage you to start studying different disci-plines—both creative and scientific. Use your discoveries in these new areas and apply them to your work. Begin to apply this formula to your process:

X works like this. What if Y worked the same way? What truths about X could we apply to Y?

Thinking this way helped me learn how to run sound at church. I imagined each cord coming into the sound board as a pipe with water flowing through it. Each knob changed the way the water moved. All pipes eventually flowed into one big pipe that fed the sound to the speakers. Understanding the movement of water illuminated the processes of electric-ity and sound.

This type of thinking will open up a brand-new world of thought and innovation for your work.

Challenge

Choose two seemingly unrelated items from the following list. Spend some time researching (if you need to) and comparing the two items. Find as many ways, in ten minutes, that these two things are similar or work in a parallel way. Now apply these similarities to problems you're facing today:

The rubber pencil magic trick
Cooking a turkey
Wave–particle duality of light
Grand jeté (ballet movement)
A lawn mower
Reductionism
A tsunami
Shadows in candlelight
Selling a used car
Taking a landscape photo

BE INCOMPARABLE

You don't need to be like other artists. God has already given you something they don't have.

Spiritual Development

For some say, "Paul's letters are demanding and forceful, but in person he is weak, and his speeches are worthless!" Those people should realize that our actions when we arrive in person will be as forceful as what we say in our letters from far away. Oh, don't worry; we wouldn't dare say that we are as wonderful as these other men who tell you how important they are! But they are only comparing themselves with each other, using themselves as the standard of measurement. How ignorant!

2 CORINTHIANS 10:10–12

I LOVE THAT PAUL was a scrapper. He wouldn't stand for people talking about him behind his back. That's the story of this section of his letter to the Corinthians.

Paul was writing instructions to the Corinthian Church—instructions on how to live up to high standards. Some folks criticized him for it. They began accusing Paul of not living up to his own principles.

They saw the way those around them were living and viewed *that* as the standard.

So Paul attacked this idea by saying how ignorant they were to compare themselves to each other. Look at it this way: while the most friendly person in a psych ward might seem great in comparison to his fellow patients, he's still unbalanced. We live in a fallen world—a madhouse. It isn't wise to compare ourselves to those around us.

So Paul is giving us a higher standard to live up to. We set our eyes, our lives to God's standards. We don't need to worry about how other people are living. We need to please God.

It's too easy to compare ourselves to those around us and feel good about ourselves. "I'm better than my neighbor." Or, "I'm better than the trash bags on reality TV." Unfortunately, normal isn't the standard by which we should measure ourselves.

I encourage you to delve into the Scriptures and see what true standards of godliness and wise living are like.

Prayer Starter

God, teach me not to compare myself to others. I want to look to Your standards of holiness and live to please You—not those around me. I know You call me to be greater, not better, in order to please You. Keep me humble as I seek to honor You and You alone.

Change the Way You Think

Just like it's unhealthy to compare ourselves to others and think we're doing well, it's unwise to compare ourselves to others and think less of ourselves.

Too many people beat themselves up thinking they need to be like those around them. Maybe they have less skill, less charisma, less outward beauty.

In 1 Samuel 18:8–9, Saul starts comparing himself to David. Not wise: "'They credit David with ten thousands and me with only thousands. Next they'll be making him their king!' So from that time on Saul kept a jealous eye on David."

Saul was being ridiculous: he was already king! Not only was he king, this young David admired him. He wasn't a threat. He was an ally.

When Saul saw the accolades and praises others lavished on David, he felt inadequate. He neglected to see what he truly had—the whole kingdom!

We need to stop looking to other people and see what God has given us as artists. God might have given you a kingdom to rule. Embrace it!

Challenge

Turn off your media today. Go Facebook silent. Go Twitter silent. Go television silent. Close yourself up to outside influences. Get rid of those things you compare yourself to and try to make something free from that. Create something today just for the enjoyment. Make something you are happy about. Don't worry about making something you'd be proud to show others.

Work on the project until you are satisfied—not your family, friends, or employers—when *you* are satisfied.

Now find an audience. Publish it anonymously on a blog. Publish it to a forum you don't frequent. Escape the normal comparisons that trap you, and find a new outlet of feedback.

You'll be inspired by the unique insight you gain.

BE DIFFERENT

Stuck in a rut? Do something different. True change requires it.

Spiritual Development

Then we turned and set out for the wilderness by the way to the Red Sea, as the Lord spoke to me, and circled Mount Seir for many days. And the Lord spoke to me, saying, "You have circled this mountain long enough. Now turn north . . . "

DEUTERONOMY 2:1–3 (NASB)

THE ISRAELITES WANDERED IN the desert for forty years. They disobeyed God, so He wouldn't let them into the land He prepared for them.

Forty years—that's a long time to be stuck as nomads. I enjoy jumping into my own bed after a long journey. These guys didn't have that luxury. Horrible.

Now it was time to finally go into the country God promised them. They began moving but circled the same mountain for many days. They were still wandering aimlessly. Finally, God told them it was time to move, go north—do something different so they could get the results they wanted.

Many Christians wander in their lives. They don't have an aim or a plan. Sure, they have a big vision for their lives, but they don't take any steps toward that vision.

I love this quote from Albert Einstein: "Insanity: doing the same thing over and over again and expecting different results."

So many of us live insane lives. We want different results but aren't willing to change our routines. We want to get our finances in order but refuse to stop eating out or making impulse buys for those electronics or new shoes. We want an over-the-top relationship but don't do over-the-top things to make it happen.

Change requires doing something different. It's as simple as that.

What do you want to see changed in your life? What steps do you need to take to see that change? Are you willing to take those steps?

Prayer Starter

God, I don't want to wander aimlessly through life. Help me learn from the story of the Israelites in the desert. Show me what steps I need to take to live an extraordinary life— one that honors and reflects You. Then give me the strength and resolve to make those changes.

Change the Way You Think

How do you feel about your work lately? Do you feel stuck? Do you feel like you're making the same things over and over?

Change requires doing something different. That means you need to change up your routine if you're stuck in a rut. The fastest way to change the direction of your work is to change the direction of your life. Change your surroundings. Change your schedule. Just change something.

We all draw inspiration from our surroundings. Have you identified what, specifically, inspires you throughout the day? At some point we need to change up our inspirations if we want to change up our work.

Maybe that means reading some different magazines. Maybe that means taking a class at a local art college. Maybe that means visiting a different Starbucks.

Whatever you can do to change your routine will help change the things you make. Change requires doing something different. Do something different.

Challenge

Get some elevation. Locate the highest accessible point in your city. Climb the building, tree, or mountain and do your creation up there. Allow the views and different perspective to inspire you.

Now work on something that reflects that altitude. Look for ways to infuse that perspective into your work. Maybe that means a rotated image if you're a graphic designer. Maybe that means dancing horizontally instead of vertically. Maybe that means writing a song about heights and depths.

Draw as much inspiration from the height as possible. Then repeat this at the lowest point in your city.

BE ASSOCIATED

> *He who walks with the creative grows creative.*

Spiritual Development

"So be very careful to follow everything Moses wrote in the Book of Instruction. Do not deviate from it, turning either to the right or to the left. Make sure you do not associate with the other people still remaining in the land. Do not even mention the names of their gods, much less swear by them or serve them or worship them. Rather, cling tightly to the LORD your God as you have done until now.

"For the LORD has driven out great and powerful nations for you, and no one has yet been able to defeat you. Each one of you will put to flight a thousand of the enemy, for the LORD your God fights for you, just as he has promised. So be very careful to love the LORD your God.

"But if you turn away from him and cling to the customs of the survivors of these nations remaining among you, and if you intermarry with them, then know for certain that the LORD your God will no longer drive them out of your land. Instead, they will

> be a snare and a trap to you, a whip for your backs
> and thorny brambles in your eyes, and you will van-
> ish from this good land the LORD your God has given
> you."
>
> JOSHUA 23:6–13

AFTER WANDERING IN THE desert for forty years, the nation of Israel finished a supernatural conquest.

With the conquest over, the invading Israelites could sit back and relax—enjoy the fruit of their hard work.

This is when God warned them: "Be careful not to get friendly with the locals. You may live in their land, but you aren't one of them. You're different."

It's impossible to not be affected by those you associate with—you become like them.

That's why it's important who we marry, who we befriend, and who we associate with—whether in person, through television, movies, books, or other media.

We lose our godly edge when we get too interlinked with the wrong people. We become like those we hang around. We find ourselves using language we shouldn't use, thinking thoughts we shouldn't think, and behaving in ways that dishonor our relationship with the Lord.

So who do you associate with? What movies and TV shows do you associate with? What musicians do you associate with? Have you lost your godly edge? Maybe it's time to get it back.

Prayer Starter

God, show me who You want me to hang around. I want to keep my godly edge. I don't want to be influenced by the wrong people in my life. Help me see opportunities for godly relationships and associations that will motivate me to live the life You have for me.

Change the Way You Think

Just like hanging around the wrong people can bring you down, hanging around the right people can lift you up. If you want to take your work and creative prowess to the next level, you need to associate with the right people.

You need mentors who will inspire you to greatness. You need someone to challenge you—to help you take your skills beyond their current state.

Too often our ruts come about when we've plateaued among our peers. When we've learned all we can from our current associates, it's easy to stop growing.

That's why we need to seek out new friendships, look for new books, find artists that will motivate us to greatness, and regain a creative edge by hanging out with creatively edgy people. Creativity—even if your work is "non-creative" by nature—will help you take your work to the next level.

Proverbs 13:20 says, "Walk with the wise and become wise." It's just as true that if you walk with the creative, you become creative.

Challenge

Identify a person in your life that annoys you. Perhaps a coworker, neighbor, customer, spouse . . . ? Identify what it is about them that annoys you. Now look for a way to turn that around on them and annoy them. What invention can you create to annoy them?

Let me illustrate it with this story. There was a certain chef making French-fried potatoes. He sent them out, but the customer sent them back. They were too thick. The chef sliced them thinner, sent them out to the customer. They came back, still too thick. The chef got annoyed. So he looked for a way to spite the diner. He sliced potatoes ultra thin and sent them out. They were a hit! The customer loved them. Thus, the potato chip was invented.

An attempt to annoy a customer yielded a truly creative result. So I ask you: who can you annoy today?

DAY 23

BE DETERMINED

> *The source of your greatest breakthrough may be a bit of sweat and determination.*

Spiritual Development

Don't you realize that in a race everyone runs, but only one person gets the prize? So run to win! All athletes are disciplined in their training. They do it to win a prize that will fade away, but we do it for an eternal prize. So I run with purpose in every step. I am not just shadowboxing. I discipline my body like an athlete, training it to do what it should. Otherwise, I fear that after preaching to others I myself might be disqualified.

1 CORINTHIANS 9:24–27

I HATE EXERCISING. I do it because I need to—otherwise I get what my wife and I like to call chunked. To get the result I want, I have to do something unpleasant. Even when I don't feel like it, I get up and go for a run. I do what's right regardless of how I feel.

That's what Paul's talking about in this passage. He talks like he's training for the Olympics. He made his body his slave so he would live the life he was called to live. He didn't feel like going to prison for his faith or teaching even when folks were threatening to stone him. He did what was right regardless of how he felt.

Paul could have spent his days enjoying the trashy reality programming of their day—The Real Gladiators of Rome. But he determined to live an exceptional life for God. He responded to God's calling.

Even though it meant some unpleasantness, it's safe to say Paul got the results he aimed for. He brought many people to Christ and communicated most of the doctrine we teach today in our churches. He couldn't have done that without subjecting his body to proper training.

God calls us to live exceptional lives too. And that will take some training—some bodily subjugation. We probably won't face prison sentences or projectile stones. But it might mean forgoing the *Real Housewives* marathons. It might mean getting up a bit early to pray. It might mean telling the truth even when it hurts. It might mean choosing a job with less compensation to be the father or mother God called us to be.

We're in a race. And the prize isn't flimsy and fleeting like a gold ribbon or a dainty crown. We run for an eternal prize. Now train for it.

Prayer Starter

Help me remember the race I'm running. I want to keep a perspective on eternity and train my mind, body, and soul for that race. I want to live an exceptional life and fully grab hold of the calling You have for me. I don't want to waste my life. Help me live extraordinarily.

Change the Way You Think

Paul didn't necessarily find immediate joy in his self-training. He wasn't a masochist. But some translations say this verse more harshly. They conjure up visions of Paul beating himself black and blue instead of giving in to temptation and sin. That's hard-core. He felt one way, but he wouldn't give in to those feelings. He powered through them.

I believe we all have situations we need to power through: motivation blocks.

There are times I approach my figurative canvas and just don't feel like it. I'm not motivated. I don't feel particularly inspired. It's easy for me to sit around and wait for inspiration to come. That probably means getting caught up in a *Real Housewives* marathon.

These times call for some Olympic-style training. We need to power through the motivation block, power through the feelings, power through the fact that we just aren't feeling it today.

You can do it! In fact, I'm doing it right now as I write this. Power through.

Challenge

Give yourself some playtime today. No matter how busy you are, block off one or two hours for creative play. You aren't going to use anything you make within this window. It's a time to experiment, play, and fail. Make something completely useless or explore an idea that will never come to anything. Don't do any real work within this window.

Keep track of this time. Write down the ideas, save the results, and catalogue it for future use. Though there probably won't be any tangible, real fruit from this exercise, it will recharge you. And who knows—one of those bad ideas might turn into something amazing.

BE LONG-SUFFERING

Great things are a result of successfully enduring pain.

Spiritual Development

Now that their father was dead, Joseph's brothers became fearful. "Now Joseph will show his anger and pay us back for all the wrong we did to him," they said.

So they sent this message to Joseph: "Before your father died, he instructed us to say to you: 'Please forgive your brothers for the great wrong they did to you—for their sin in treating you so cruelly.' So we, the servants of the God of your father, beg you to forgive our sin." When Joseph received the message, he broke down and wept. Then his brothers came and threw themselves down before Joseph. "Look, we are your slaves!" they said.

But Joseph replied, "Don't be afraid of me. Am I God, that I can punish you? You intended to harm me, but God intended it all for good. He brought me to this position so I could save the lives of many people."

GENESIS 50:15–20

IN CASE YOU DON'T know the story, Joseph's brothers were a jealous lot. Because he was their father's favorite, they sold him into slavery. Talk about the ultimate betrayal.

They assumed Joseph was dead or rotting away across the world as a slave. But Joseph, through a set of crummy situations and crazy stories, rose to the second most powerful position in Egypt. Later, his brothers were forced to go to Egypt to seek food due to a famine in Israel.

His brothers feared Joseph was going to punish them. But he didn't. He didn't even really blame them. He knew the bad situations and his response to them led him to his position. He acknowledged that the pain he endured was a good thing. That pain prepared him to rule a nation.

Many of us want to rule nations. Perhaps not literal nations, but we want to be significant. We want to make a difference. Yet we also shy away from life's pains like they're bad things.

We want to rise in the kingdom without going through the pain it takes to get there. Very few people are simply handed greatness. They endured trials to get there. Pain is a necessary step on the road to greatness.

Regardless of whether or not the pain you endure is self-inflicted, random, or prompted by God, your response will either lead you toward greatness or away from it. The first step of responding well is to embrace it. See it as an opportunity.

The right response: Learn and grow through pain. The wrong response: Whining, complaining, and blaming God.

How will you respond to the pain in your life?

Prayer Starter

God, I realize from the moment of birth, pain is part of life. Help me respond properly to it, see Your hand in it, and embrace it. Teach me to respond appropriately to situations I find less than favorable. I pray that, instead of blaming You, I will look to You for comfort and strength to endure.

Change the Way You Think

It's a huge temptation for us to look at successful people and get jealous. They may have the notoriety, clients or skills we want. Unfortunately we also don't see the development process they went through to get where they are.

While we should always strive to become better at our craft and take hold of new opportunities, it's also important that we learn to embrace the growth process.

Many of the most public successes went through the deepest pits in their careers. If you look back ten years, you wouldn't be so quick to want to switch places with them.

Those bad situations were the things that gave them the character and skills to cope with the new pressures their notoriety brought.

It's not all golden at the top. The higher you rise, the further you fall if you don't have the foundation that pain and struggle bring. Don't be like the disgraced politician in his scandal, who neglected the development of character along with his rise to power.

Challenge

Create a set of directions for yourself, without knowing your destination or starting point. Write the directions on a paper like this:

1. Drive one mile and turn right at the first available turn.

2. Take the next available left.

3. Take a U-turn and drive .5 miles.

4. Take the fifth right.

Choose your own random directions. Then get in your car, drive to the center of your town, and follow your directions. It's okay if you get lost (you might want to bring a GPS). Enjoy the journey, then get out of your car at your destination. Explore. Take pictures. See what different sights you can see.

BE SECURE

Murder that voice of insecurity.

Spiritual Development

And I heard a loud voice in heaven, saying, "Now the salvation and the power and the kingdom of our God and the authority of his Christ have come, for the accuser of our brothers has been thrown down, who accuses them day and night before our God. And they have conquered him by the blood of the Lamb and by the word of their testimony, for they loved not their lives even unto death. Therefore, rejoice, O heavens and you who dwell in them! But woe to you, O earth and sea, for the devil has come down to you in great wrath, because he knows that his time is short!"

REVELATION 12:10–12 (ESV)

WE'VE ALL HEARD WE shouldn't be judgmental of others. That's true. Remove the log from your own eye before you worry about the speck in another's eye. Rarely do you hear that you shouldn't be so judgmental of yourself.

Follow me here. I'm not saying you should pat yourself on the back when you sin. I'm not saying to overlook your flaws. I am saying that, after you fail, get yourself up, dust yourself off, and keep moving forward.

In this passage, the accuser of our brothers refers to Satan. He's constantly accusing us to God and to ourselves—saying we aren't good enough. He's the one trying to keep you down when you fail. He's whispering, "You'll never be good enough. Just stay down. Stop trying."

An even quieter voice is whispering, "Get back up. I'm with you in this. Keep trying." Even more, Jesus is answering the devil, defending us—through His work on the cross.

You'll never be good enough to earn God's love, but that doesn't matter. God is behind you, encouraging you to keep going, and loves you because of who He is—not because of anything you do or don't do. We don't need to accuse ourselves and beat ourselves up—someone else is already filling that role adequately. Don't steal that role.

Press on. Forget what is behind. Don't let past failures keep you from forward progress.

Prayer Starter

God, I fail. Daily. I don't want that to keep me from moving in the direction You have for me. I know You defend me when Satan accuses me. I pray I won't give in to the temptation to beat myself up when I fail. You forgave me for every sin and shortcoming before I was even born. Free me from guilt and condemnation, and help me live a life of forward progress. Remind me there is no condemnation for those in Christ Jesus.

Change the Way You Think

You're probably all too familiar with that voice that whispers: you aren't good enough. While it may not be Satan in the case of your work, the voice can be just as scary. It can keep you stuck in a rut or fearful of making something of consequence.

Everyone has that voice in their head—even the successful people you admire. They've found a way to suppress that voice and move forward with their work. You can't listen to that voice. You need to put it down and move forward. Shut down your internal insecurities and create.

Your insecurity will always be your biggest obstacle to making something—especially to creating something that matters. Typically the more important a project, the more our insecurity grips us. Those are the times it's important to persevere.

I love this quote from George Lois (nicknamed Mr. Big Idea), posted on the blog *Swiss Miss* on November 21, 2012: "Onwards and upwards, and never give your failures a second thought."

Challenge

There are twenty-six letters in the English language. But there are far more than twenty-six sounds. As many people before you have attempted, pick a sound for which there is no letter and create a twenty-seventh letter for the English language. Draw it out. Make that letter unique from other letters in the English language, and make it represent a certain sound. For instance: "sh," "ct," "gr."

Create a lowercase and uppercase version of this new letter.

This is an incredibly daunting task and may evoke feelings of insecurity. Go for it anyway. Then share your new letter with your friends on Twitter, Facebook, or Instagram.

BE DEFEATED

Great people aren't born great.
They're chiseled into greatness.

Spiritual Development

"Simon, Simon, behold, Satan demanded to have you, that he might sift you like wheat, but I have prayed for you that your faith may not fail. And when you have turned again, strengthen your brothers." Peter said to him, "Lord, I am ready to go with you both to prison and to death." Jesus said, "I tell you, Peter, the rooster will not crow this day, until you deny three times that you know me."

LUKE 22:31–34 (ESV)

FAILURE IS THE WORST. It feels horrible to fail.

Here you have a situation where Jesus tells Peter he's going to fail. Satan wanted to mess with Peter. Then Jesus tells Peter, "I've prayed for you."

At that moment, I imagine Peter lets out a sigh of relief. He's thinking, "Good, Jesus won't let Satan cause me to stumble. I won't fail because my homeboy will keep it from happening."

But no. Jesus says, "After you fail miserably, I'll help you get back up, and you're going to be able to strengthen those around you."

How confusing that had to be for Peter. Peter doesn't want to fail. Failure is bad. But Jesus doesn't seem too concerned with it. Jesus is willing to let Peter fail—He's happy with the end result.

I'm convinced failure is necessary. No matter what the failure, if we learn from it, we're propelled forward—even the really bad stuff.

Peter was about to deny Jesus three times! That's close to an ultimate failure in my book. Jesus didn't try to stop it. He knew, in the end, Peter would be stronger for it. He knew Peter could get back up, and that he'd grow as a result of his failure.

We don't just *go* through failure, we can *grow* through failure.

That means you can try something bold for God. You can take a huge risk and know that, failure or success, good things will happen in your life. God's more concerned with conforming you to the image of Christ than you living a flawless life.

Be bold for God.

Prayer Starter

God, I know You work even through bad situations. When I fail, You use that as an opportunity to conform me to the image of Christ. Don't let me fear failure. I want to take big, God-honoring risks. I know when I do You won't leave me on my own. You'll pick me up if I fall, and You'll teach me, bringing me to a new level of glory with You.

Change the Way You Think

You need to give yourself room to fail in your work. How can someone progress if they have never failed?

Great people aren't born great. They're chiseled into greatness. Failure, bumps, and falls smooth their edges and make them something better than the original product.

I want to encourage you to embrace failure—not just as a necessary evil, but as an awesome opportunity. The one thing all great people have in common is failure. Abraham Lincoln, one of America's most beloved presidents, failed countless times before becoming president. He lost eight elections and suffered a nervous breakdown that confined him to his bed for six months in 1836.

Even athletes embrace failure—in basketball, a 50 percent shooting average is considered great. Imagine if we allowed ourselves to fail half the time and still considered ourselves successful. We'd probably create a lot more and risk even bigger things.

Just remember that failure isn't ultimately failure. It's an opportunity to learn, adjust, and try again.

Challenge

Pick an artistic discipline you know very little or nothing about. Now take thirty minutes to an hour and create something truly epic with that medium. Don't spend too much time with details, but go over the top.

Examples:

Write an epic love song—the best love song in the history of the world.

Write a short story in which your hero single-handedly saves the world.

Create an epic feast using ingredients you've never used.

Take the best photo in the history of the world.

You'll probably fail—miserably. But you'll find yourself laughing at the crazy ideas and techniques you come up with. Who knows, you might stumble upon something very useful.

BE GENEROUS

> *Great work comes from life,*
> *and life is best when*
> *we give to others.*

Spiritual Development

**Remember: A stingy planter gets a stingy crop; a
lavish planter gets a lavish crop. I want each of you
to take plenty of time to think it over, and make up
your own mind what you will give. That will protect
you against sob stories and arm-twisting. God loves
it when the giver delights in the giving.**

2 CORINTHIANS 9:6–7 (MSG)

PASTORS ARE GOOD AT applying verses like this to finances.
While this verse is about finances, there's a deeper principle
in this text.

"A lavish planter gets a lavish crop." That concept applies to everything in our life. It isn't just saying those who

give money generously get money generously. It's talking about giving anything.

My favorite example of this is a smile. Walk down a busy street and scowl at people. They'll scowl back. But if you put a smile on your face, you'll notice people smiling back. You gave a smile but received twenty more. You planted joy and reaped it back.

This concept applies to so many areas in our life. What do we want to get back from people?

Do we want to be respected? Why don't we try giving others respect—even when they don't deserve it. Respond respectfully to your boss. To that guy who cut you off. Even to the IRS agent that's auditing you. It may seem like a huge sacrifice, and it won't always work, but we'll get back respect by the bucketful.

What about friendship? If we want friends, be friendly. Go out of our way to serve others. Be there for them. Love the unlovable. It always comes back.

The principle works because God set it up. Even the act of the cross was sowing and reaping on Jesus' part. While we were still sinners, Christ died for us. He sowed love into us even when we didn't deserve it. His loves for us encourages us to love Him back.

He gave something He wanted back from us—He gave His life because He wanted ours in return. He set up the principle. It works. Even He abides by it.

So what do you want from life? Are you willing to give it to receive it?

Prayer Starter

God, teach me to be generous in life. I know You've set up the principle of sowing and reaping to teach me generosity. You have good things in store for me; You're just waiting for me to start giving the things I have. I want to give love, respect, assistance, and friendship to those around me—knowing You have even more coming back to me.

Change the Way You Think

Some of your best ideas will come when you're helping others with their projects. I'm sure you've experienced this. You're brainstorming with a friend and you come up with an obvious solution. As you think about it more, you realize that solution works for some of your problems too. It's uncanny. That's the power of community.

I'm sure there's a deep psychological reason this works. I believe God set us up to work best when we're helping others. We were meant to work in community.

Unfortunately some people—specifically artists—tend to be bad at the whole community thing. We like to sit in our dark rooms with paint and a canvas, and create. Sometimes we even get morbid about how much our art consumes us.

I encourage you to find a group of like-minded people and start creating life with them. Start a community of free-flowing ideas and support. Invest in these friends and let them invest back in you. Even if they work in different industries or mediums than yours, link up. It's worth it.

You don't have to be lonely.

Challenge

Take a moment today and solve one of the world's smaller problems. Seriously, take a problem humans struggle with and find a creative solution. It doesn't necessarily have to work flawlessly or even be serious, but get your brain thinking bigger than your small (by comparison) problems.

Here are some problems you can take a crack at solving:

- Childhood obesity
- Bad drivers
- Grumpy senior citizens
- Nickelback

BE DEDICATED

> *Creativity is an endless mountain we'll never summit.*

Spiritual Development

Now the Lord is the Spirit, and where the Spirit of the Lord is present, there is freedom. And we all, with unveiled faces reflecting the glory of the Lord, are being transformed into the same image from one degree of glory to another, which is from the Lord, who is the Spirit.

2 CORINTHIANS 3:17–18 (NET)

Do you remember standardized test days in grade school? Did you get nervous? You'd sit at the desk, number-2 pencil in hand, hoping to pass the impossible test that showed you weren't a loser bound to repeat the second grade for the rest of your life.

Perhaps it wasn't that dramatic, but we feel like that sometimes in life. God gives us a test and we bomb—we fail.

We've all failed life's tests. Sins, habits, unhealthy behaviors. We fail and we fail often.

It can make you feel like the Christian life is hopeless.

Let me offer you this encouragement. God's not going to fail you even if you fail the same test two thousand times. He doesn't mind retakes. His ultimate goal is to conform you into the image of Christ. He doesn't have a time line for that.

The best part: if you're seeking God, no matter how often you fail, you will eventually be conformed into the image of Christ. "We know that when He appears, we will be like Him, because we will see Him just as He is" (1 John 3:2 NASB).

When we die, the work will be done. We'll be handed life's diploma. We'll be like Christ when we see Christ.

This isn't an excuse to be lazy. This isn't a *sit-back-and-relax* message. It is a *don't-give-up-hope* message.

Do your best to pass the tests, but rely on Him for the grade. When you fail, don't beat yourself up. You'll have the opportunity to pass next time. If you fail the rest of your life but are seeking God with your whole heart, you're going to make it. You'll be like Him, because you'll see Him as He is.

Prayer Starter

God, give me the grace to pass the tests You put before me. When I fail, give me the grace to get back up and try again. I know Your goal is that I'm conformed into the image of Jesus. You have the patience to see that happen, I pray You'd give me that same patience. We both know it's going to be a very long road—but one worth traveling.

Change the Way You Think

My favorite part of the passage in 2 Corinthians is the "one degree of glory to another" part (ESV). Another translation (KJV) says God takes us "from glory to glory."

I like to think of creativity as a mountain. I feel like I'll reach the peak. I'll hit the summit. I will have conquered creativity. That's somewhat comforting to me—thinking I'll finally reach a destination. It's also a bit depressing. What if I reach the peak and stop developing? What if I plateau? Plateauing would mean I'm forever doomed to the same patterns, the same methods, and the same relationships. Without creativity in my life nothing would change.

Fortunately, it isn't that way. It's a glory to glory situation. Once you hit one peak, there's a new peak waiting. You can climb the mountain of creativity forever. That's a great thing.

Embrace that truth. You'll never reach the top. But also don't forget the distance you've already scaled.

When you're looking forward on your climb, it's sometimes hard to see progress. Continually running into new mountains can be discouraging. So it's important to acknowledge the climbing you've already done. As you scale this mountain of creativity, I encourage you to look back occasionally and see the progress you've made. Take a moment and reflect on where you've been. Don't dwell on the previous climb, but don't forget it either.

Challenge

Break free from a thought-plateau today and keep climbing the mountain of creativity by asking a big "what if?" question. Expand your mind to new possibilities and explore.

Write a short story based on this seed idea: What if the Mars rover came across a house on Mars—with an American flag waving outside?

Answer these questions: Who lives there? How did they get there? What do they do? Who or what do they interact with? Are they alone?

Explore, explore, and explore some more.

BE BOLD

> *To make something new you need to risk . . . a lot—your ego, your reputation, your time.*

Spiritual Development

Trust in the Lord with all your heart; do not depend on your own understanding. Seek his will in all you do, and he will show you which path to take.

PROVERBS 3:5–6

The wicked run away when no one is chasing them, but the godly are as bold as lions.

PROVERBS 28:1

So humble yourselves under the mighty power of God, and at the right time he will lift you up in honor.

1 PETER 5:6

DO YOU REMEMBER SWIMMING at the community pool as a kid? You were probably nervous to jump in, right? Even though your mom fitted you with floaties and sunscreen, you were afraid you'd drown if you took the plunge.

That is, until your dad hopped in. He'd stand in the pool and beckon you to jump. "It's going to be fine. I'll catch you."

You were safe. You knew you could jump in and your dad would catch you. No matter what, you were safe because your dad was there for you.

That's the assurance we have with God. If He's telling us to jump into something, we can be sure He won't let us drown—no matter how deep the water. We can take the plunge knowing He'll catch us.

When we humble ourselves, trust God, and seek His will in all we do, we know we're safe. It doesn't matter if God calls us to literally jump in a pool or sell all we have and move to the Amazon rainforest. God will keep us from drowning.

The coolest thing about all this is that God calls us to be bold. So often we think the Christian life is a wimpy, quiet life. But if we humble ourselves and trust in God, we can do crazy, risky things for Him. We can risk the glorious, knowing we're safe.

So what has God called you to do? Have you been afraid to step out? Don't just stand at the side of the pool dipping your big toe in the water. Plunge in. It might be scary. You might even sink a little. But at the right time you'll feel the Hands of Protection lifting you up.

Prayer Starter

God, I don't want to live a safe life. I want to be bold. I know when I humble myself, trust in You, and seek Your will, there is so much protection. God I believe You'll protect me. Help me overcome my unbelief.

Change the Way You Think

Great innovators are bold. They risk. They put aside their fear and take a leap into the unknown.

This is what the great filmmaker Francis Ford Coppola said about risk in an interview by Ariston Anderson for the website 99u.com:

"Even in the early days of the movies, they didn't know how to make movies. They had an image and it moved and the audience loved it. You saw a train coming into the station, and just to see motion was beautiful. The cinema language happened by experimentation—by people not knowing what to do."

There are too many people mimicking what they see. Designers copy design styles, musicians stick with genre formulas, authors mimic bestsellers. The world needs new. The world needs your new.

How will you risk to make something new?

Challenge

Throughout the day, as you work on your projects, ask yourself some random "what if?" questions. There's an appendix at the end of the book filled with them. Make copies, cut them into slivers of paper, then stick them in a jar, and draw one every hour. (Set a timer if you need to.)

BE LIGHT

> *We were created to show others our perspective using creative methods.*

Spiritual Development

"Let me tell you why you are here. You're here to be salt-seasoning that brings out the God-flavors of this earth. If you lose your saltiness, how will people taste godliness? You've lost your usefulness and will end up in the garbage.

"Here's another way to put it: You're here to be light, bringing out the God-colors in the world. God is not a secret to be kept. We're going public with this, as public as a city on a hill. If I make you light-bearers, you don't think I'm going to hide you under a bucket, do you? I'm putting you on a light stand. Now that I've put you there on a hilltop, on a light stand—shine! Keep open house; be generous with your lives. By opening up to others, you'll prompt people to open up with God, this generous Father in heaven."

MATTHEW 5:13–16 (MSG)

I LOVE THIS PASSAGE. What are we put on this earth to do? We're here to be salt. We're here to be light.

What does light do? It lets people see things they couldn't see before. We live in a dark world. People don't see God even though He's all around them. Our job is to make Him visible to others.

There's this popular idea in Christendom that we can be a witness through art—that by creating beautiful things, we're letting the world see God. Though there may be some validity to this, we can use it as a serious cop out.

The truth is: our lives are the light. Not what we make. When we're generous with others, when we stay undimmed by the pollution and scuzz of the world—that's what it means to shine your light.

It's wonderful to create beautiful art and let God's love shine through it. However, if we neglect to let God's love shine through us, we're missing God's ultimate goal for our lives.

Prayer Starter

God, I want to be salt and light to the world like You created me to be. Help me live a generous life, free from the world's pollution. I want people to see You through me. I pray I'd be transparent and You'd be visible. May I become less and You become greater.

Change the Way You Think

When God spoke and said, "Let there be light," He made it possible for us to explore and to see what He sees in His creative art. His creative initiative lights the world.

That's true creative power. That's what creativity is all about—showing others what you see. That's what an artist does. "Let me show you the possibilities I see"—illumination.

When God made us in His own image, we were meant to illuminate. Just as He is the light, He created us to be light. He wants us to show others what we've seen, to bear witness to the creativity we find around us.

Creativity isn't some excessively complicated thing. It's simple. Just show others what you see.

Sometimes we make it so complicated. We spend late nights praying for inspiration. We get depressed when our creative light isn't shining brightly enough.

It need not be so excruciating. We just need to show people what we see. You see things others never could. Simply illuminate that. Your creative light will shine.

Challenge

Combine any three objects from List A. Use those three objects to invent two or three contraptions from List B. Your job in this challenge is to see the possibilities in these objects. Use your imagination and see past their literal uses to their potential; let your creative light shine. (Feel free to destroy these objects if you need to.)

Then take that mindset and apply it to your projects today.

List A:	List B:
Paper clip	Mouse trap
Rubber band	Projectile weapon
Ballpoint pen	Instrument capable of
Coffee mug	multiple tones/notes
Sugar packet	Work of art
Business card	Functional tablet/phone
Headphones	accessory
Coffee stirrer	Magic trick
Hair clip/bobby pin	Picture holder/frame

50 WHAT IFS

1. What if you incorporated a bomb into this work? Would it make it better or worse? How would it change it?

2. What would a ninja change about this if it were his project?

3. What if this had the personality of a tasmanian devil?

4. What if you made it smaller? Bigger?

5. What if it had a superpower?

6. What would you change about this to appeal to another culture? Icelanders? Aborigines? Amish?

7. What if you were working on this in caveman times?

8. What would happen if you added fire or ice to the mix?

9. What would you change about your approach if you knew the world was ending tomorrow?

10. What if you had five times your current budget? What if you had half?

11. What if this was experienced with a different sense than usual? For example, what if you smelled a painting? What if you heard a dance? What if you only felt a meal?

12. What if you removed half of its components/elements?

13. What if God was one of us? What would He tell you to change?

14. What if you found this in space?

15. What if Bugs Bunny were creating this?

16. What if this creation were going to be featured on the Disney Channel?

17. What would a futuristic cyborg do differently?

18. What costume would your project wear for Halloween?

19. What if it was a magic trick?

20. What if a dog were working on this? How would he approach it?

21. What if you were creating this underwater?

22. What if the last person on earth consumed this project?

23. What would your creation talk about in a therapy session?

24. What if your work had a favorite song? What would it be?

25. What if the people who'd be experiencing this were twenty feet tall? What would you change to give them a better experience?

26. What if your deadline was in five minutes?

27. What if every person who experienced this work was drunk when they experienced it?

28. What if you only used your tongue/toes/nose to make this?

29. What if your only tool was sand?

30. What if you were creating for a demographic that intrinsically hates you?

31. What if your work were illegal?

32. What if you were an ant? How would you produce this?

33. What if there was a secret code/treasure map embedded in your work? Where would it lead?

34. What if your favorite artist were creating this? How would they approach it?

35. What if a novice/newbie were approaching this? What mistakes would they make?

36. What if the building you're in caught on fire? What last minute detail would you add before you stopped, dropped, and rolled?

37. What if you were creating this from inside the belly of a whale?

38. What if MacGyver were creating this?

39. What if you were making this on a deserted island and only had three primitive tools? What would they be? What if you only created with those now?

40. What if you were extremely limited? You only had two colors to work with, two chords to work with, a vocabulary of twenty words . . . ?

41. What if Kanye West interrupted you right now? What would you do differently whenever he let you finish?

42. What if you had to use at least one outdated technique to finish your project?

43. What if you couldn't use technology to produce this?

44. What if they made a movie about this time of your life? Who would play you? How would they change your work to make it more movie-friendly?

45. What if money were no object for this project?

46. What if it was made as a Barbie accessory or feature?

47. What if you had to describe this on Twitter—in 140 characters or less?

48. What if you had to incorporate Legos into this work?

49. What if this creation offended you?

50. What if you didn't finish this?

TRACKING YOUR PROGRESS

---

*How to track your progress
with fellow* Created for
More *readers.*

DO YOU WANT TO track your progress through *Created for More*? Want to see what others are getting from the book? We've set up a companion site for the book at www.createdformore.me. Submit your thoughts and challenge results through social media or directly on the site.

You can tweet or post to Instagram what you'd like to contribute. Just use the hashtag #createdformore when you post. Make sure your profile isn't set on private; otherwise our site won't be able to see what you post.

Once we verify it isn't anything offensive or off-topic, we'll approve it for the site and others will be able to see what you posted.

You can also submit directly to the site if social media isn't your cup of tea. Simply click "Submit" when you get to the site.

Feel free to peruse the site and leave comments on the pieces you like. Make friends with your fellow *Created for More* readers and get the most out of the book. It's the perfect opportunity to put Day 22 into action and connect with others.

NOTES

1. F. Scott Fitzgerald, "The Crack Up," *Esquire*. February, 1936, accessed March 2, 2013, www.esquire.com/features/ the-crack-up.

2. Westminster Assembly, *Westminster Shorter Catechism*, accessed March 13, 2013, www.reformed.org/documents/ WSC.html.

3. G. K. Chesterton, *A Miscellany of Men* (Norfolk, VA: IHS Press, 2004), 159–60.

ACKNOWLEDGMENTS

WHILE ONE PERSON GETS the credit, a book is a collection of inspiration, work, and love from countless others. I want to say a huge thank you for many who helped make this possible.

- The Moody Collective and Moody Publishers team, for countless edits, wrestling with my small-mindedness, and being generally awesome.

- The RT Creative Group team, for investing in this book initially by offering edits and support.

- My dad, Richard Malm, for pastoring me through most of my life. Many of the thoughts in this book are actually things I learned from him as he navigated his faith and his church.

- My brother, Joël, for inspiring me to write.

- My mother and sister for reminding me it's okay to be a sensitive boy, in touch with his creative side.

- My wife, Carolina, for being one of the most unintentionally creative people I know.

Other Moody Collective Books

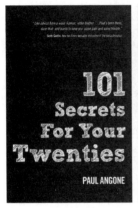

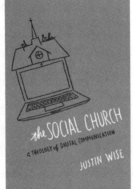

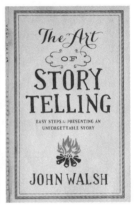

moody
collective

Join our email newsletter list to get resources and
encouragement as you build a deeper faith.

Moody Collective brings words of life to a generation seeking deeper faith. We are a part of Moody Publishers, representing this next generation of followers of Christ through books on creativity, travel, the gospel, storytelling, decision making, leadership, and more.

We seek to know, love, and serve the millennial generation with grace and humility. Each of our books is intended to challenge and encourage our readers as they pursue God.

When you sign up for our newsletter, you'll get our emails twice a month. These will include the best of the resources we've seen online, book deals and giveaways, plus behind-the-scenes and extra content from our books and authors. Sign up at *www.moodycollective.com.*

a part of Moody Publishers

Is there a gap between you and your dream?

A few years back while climbing a mountain, Joël Malm had the idea to lead people on outdoor expeditions with a spiritual, God-centered focus. Following God's lead, he created a vision map, started his organization, and made it happen.

This book is a response to the question he often gets: *How do you do something like that?* Whether you want to start a business, raise a family, run a marathon, plant a church, restore a relationship, or climb a mountain, you can take practical steps to see your vision come to be.

Vision Map is not a formula for overnight success, but it is a template to start anyone on the path to envisioning their God-given dream. God often gives us a difficult problem to solve, and we just need a push in the right direction to find the answer.

MOODYCOLLECTIVE.COM

How do you pack for all fifty states?

When I was in college, I figured my life would come together around graduation. I'd meet a guy; we'd plan a beautiful wedding and buy a nice house—not necessarily with a picket fence, but with whatever kind of fence we wanted. Whatever we decided, I would be happy.

When I got out of college and my life didn't look like that, I floundered, trying to get the life I had always dreamed of. Just when I had given up all hope of finding the "life I'd always dreamed about," I decided to take a trip to all fifty states...because when you go on a trip, you can't take your baggage. What I found was that "packing light" wasn't as easy as I thought it would be.

This is the story of my trip and learning to live life with less baggage.

MOODYCOLLECTIVE.COM

MOODYRADIO

Where you turn. For life.

Moody Radio produces and delivers compelling programs filled with biblical insights and creative expressions of faith that help you take the next step in your relationship with Christ.

You can hear Moody Radio on 36 stations and more than 1,500 radio outlets across the U.S. and Canada. Or listen on your smartphone with the Moody Radio app!

www.moodyradio.org